Microsoft System Center Configuration Manager

High availability and performance tuning

Deploy a scalable solution by ensuring high availability and disaster recovery using Configuration Manager

Marius Sandbu

[PACKT] PUBLISHING enterprise
professional expertise distilled

BIRMINGHAM - MUMBAI

Microsoft System Center Configuration Manager

High availability and performance tuning

First published: November 2013

Production Reference: 1191113

Published by Packt Publishing Ltd.
Livery Place
35 Livery Street
Birmingham B3 2PB, UK.

ISBN 978-1-78217-676-3

www.packtpub.com

Cover Image by Ravaji Babu (ravaji_babu@outlook.com)

Credits

Author
Marius Sandbu

Reviewers
Dragos Madarasan
Marius A. Skovli

Acquisition Editor
Antony Lowe

Commissioning Editor
Manasi Pandire

Technical Editors
Pragnesh Bilimoria
Iram Malik
Veena Pagare

Project Coordinator
Aboli Ambardekar

Proofreader
Mario Cecere

Indexer
Hemangini Bari

Graphics
Yuvraj Mannari

Production Coordinator
Aparna Bhagat

Cover Work
Aparna Bhagat

About the Author

Marius Sandbu is a Consultant, Advisor, and Trainer working at the VAD (Value Added Distributor) Commaxx in Norway. He has worked with Microsoft technology for over 8 years and has recently been awarded with a MVP title from Microsoft because of his high dedication to the Microsoft community. He is also a board member of the local Microsoft technology user group and spoken at many public events at both Microsoft and other events.

Marius has always had a high interest in technology, over the past few years he has taken over 20 certifications on different areas and technology, and also had a role within Microsoft as a V-TSP. He is also a certified Microsoft trainer and has held different courses, within System Center and Windows Server.

As an experiment to improve his learning skills, he started blogging in 2012 and now has over 2000 visitors to date. He also contributes to Born To Learn which is a Microsoft community website for training and certification.

I thank my lovely other half, Silje, for supporting and having patience with me, this is what made the book possible! Wouldn't be possible without you!

I also thank the people at Packt Publishing for a clean and efficient process with the book writing. It was a good experience and I've learned a lot during the process.

About the Reviewers

Dragos Madarasan is a Support Engineer for one of the fastest growing companies in Eastern Europe. After previous stints as a freelance IT Consultant and working for a Fortune 500 company, he now enjoys tackling complex scenarios and using his knowledge to bridge the space between IT and business needs.

Dragos publishes interesting cases on his personal blog and whenever time permits enjoys taking part in the ITSpark community as a Technical Writer and Speaker.

When not in front of a laptop, Dragos enjoys running and reading books on his Kindle.

Marius A. Skovli is a senior systems engineer at the consultant company Eniotec. It is a Microsoft partner specializing in delivering System Center and Windows Server solutions. He has worked with System Management since **Microsoft System Management Server (SMS) 2003** and has focused on SMS and the latest version, **System Center Configuration Manager (SCCM)**, ever since. Marius has extensive experience and knowledge of enterprise environments with high security demands, both private and governmental.

In addition to vast experience with SMS and SCCM solutions, he is also a certified MCP (SMS 2003), MCTS (SCCM 2007 / SCCM 2012), MCITP (enterprise administrator), and MCSE (private cloud).

Marius is the co-founder of Eniotec. His role is to help customers design, implement, and maintain their Configuration Manager environments. He also speaks at events and contributes on forums. In his spare time, he blogs and tweets about Microsoft System Center.

www.PacktPub.com

Support files, eBooks, discount offers and more

You might want to visit www.PacktPub.com for support files and downloads related to your book.

Did you know that Packt offers eBook versions of every book published, with PDF and ePub files available? You can upgrade to the eBook version at www.PacktPub.com and as a print book customer, you are entitled to a discount on the eBook copy. Get in touch with us at service@packtpub.com for more details.

At www.PacktPub.com, you can also read a collection of free technical articles, sign up for a range of free newsletters and receive exclusive discounts and offers on Packt books and eBooks.

PACKTLIB

`http://PacktLib.PacktPub.com`

Do you need instant solutions to your IT questions? PacktLib is Packt's online digital book library. Here, you can access, read and search across Packt's entire library of books.

Why Subscribe?

- Fully searchable across every book published by Packt
- Copy and paste, print and bookmark content
- On demand and accessible via web browser

Free Access for Packt account holders

If you have an account with Packt at www.PacktPub.com, you can use this to access PacktLib today and view nine entirely free books. Simply use your login credentials for immediate access.

Instant Updates on New Packt Books

Get notified! Find out when new books are published by following @PacktEnterprise on Twitter, or the *Packt Enterprise* Facebook page.

Table of Contents

Preface

Microsoft System Center Configuration Manager is a book that covers all of the aspects from planning to deploying a redundant Configuration Manager environment.

What this book covers

Chapter 1, Planning for High Availability with Configuration Manager, covers what you need to plan for when you want to set up High Availability for your site. For instance, it shows how to plan a layout for SQL Server, what kind of networking technology to use, and so on.

Chapter 2, Configuring Roles for High Availability, covers how you can deploy the different Configuration Manager roles that are highly available. For instance, it shows how we can deploy the application catalog service redundantly and the different forms of distribution points, and how they can affect the performance on our site.

Chapter 3, Deploy Highly Available Backend Services, covers how you can deploy backend services, such as DNS and AD that are highly available and how they operate together. It will also cover services such as SQL and using a redundant PKI solution.

Chapter 4, Backup and Recovery, covers what you need to take into account and how you can back up and restore a Configuration Manager environment. It also covers how the content store is built up and what we can use to back it up.

Chapter 5, Performance Tuning, covers various performance tuning tips such as OS deployment, virtualized environments, and SQL deployments. This chapter will also go into different OS tuning tips such as identifying bottlenecks using different tools.

What you need for this book

In order to try out the subjects covered in this book, it is recommended to download an evaluation version of Configuration Manager VHD from Microsoft, which can be found at `http://www.microsoft.com/en-us/download/details.aspx?id=36428`. It contains a preconfigured Configuration Manager site with SQL and AD. It is also recommended to use a virtualized environment when evaluating technologies such as Hyper-V, VMware workstation, or Virtual box in a local environment.

Who this book is for

This book is for IT professionals who are or have been working with Configuration Manager and those wish to learn more about deploying a redundant and scalable solution. This book is also suitable for people that wish to learn more about Configuration Manager outside its basic functions.

Conventions

In this book, you will find a number of styles of text that distinguish between different kinds of information. Here are some examples of these styles, and an explanation of their meaning.

New terms and **important words** are shown in bold. Words that you see on the screen, in menus or dialog boxes for example, appear in the text like this: "clicking on the **Next** button moves you to the next screen".

> Warnings or important notes appear in a box like this.

> Tips and tricks appear like this.

Reader feedback

Feedback from our readers is always welcome. Let us know what you think about this book—what you liked or may have disliked. Reader feedback is important for us to develop titles that you really get the most out of.

To send us general feedback, simply send an e-mail to `feedback@packtpub.com`, and mention the book title via the subject of your message.

If there is a topic that you have expertise in and you are interested in either writing or contributing to a book, see our author guide on `www.packtpub.com/authors`.

Customer support

Now that you are the proud owner of a Packt book, we have a number of things to help you to get the most from your purchase.

Errata

Although we have taken every care to ensure the accuracy of our content, mistakes do happen. If you find a mistake in one of our books—maybe a mistake in the text or the code—we would be grateful if you would report this to us. By doing so, you can save other readers from frustration and help us improve subsequent versions of this book. If you find any errata, please report them by visiting `http://www.packtpub.com/submit-errata`, selecting your book, clicking on the **errata submission form** link, and entering the details of your errata. Once your errata are verified, your submission will be accepted and the errata will be uploaded on our website, or added to any list of existing errata, under the Errata section of that title. Any existing errata can be viewed by selecting your title from `http://www.packtpub.com/support`.

Piracy

Piracy of copyright material on the Internet is an ongoing problem across all media. At Packt, we take the protection of our copyright and licenses very seriously. If you come across any illegal copies of our works, in any form, on the Internet, please provide us with the location address or website name immediately so that we can pursue a remedy.

Please contact us at `copyright@packtpub.com` with a link to the suspected pirated material.

We appreciate your help in protecting our authors, and our ability to bring you valuable content.

Questions

You can contact us at `questions@packtpub.com` if you are having a problem with any aspect of the book, and we will do our best to address it.

1

Planning for High Availability with Configuration Manager

Configuration Manager can be a complex solution to grasp, as it can span from thousands to tens of thousands of different clients placed all around the globe on different platforms. And with the large number of features it contains, it also requires a well-planned infrastructure in place to serve all the different clients.

The whole concept of a system being highly available is that a service (or services) will still be available to serve the users in case of a general failure of a single component or components in the infrastructure. If a system is not Highly Available and a critical component goes offline, your service might go offline, and depending on the priority and **service level agreement** (**SLA**) of that service, this situation might be damaging for the entire business and its users.

And of course you always want to plan ahead to make sure your solution is available at all times to serve your users. We will begin by going through the various components that makes up a Configuration Manager site and how they work to serve the clients.

In this chapter we will be covering the following topics:

- Planning for High Availability
- Different roles and components within Configuration Manager
- Planning for database configuration
- Network usage Configuration Manager
- What's new with Service Pack 1

Planning

When planning for High Availability you need to look at every aspect of your infrastructure; spanning from the underlying hardware to the software running on top of the different servers that serve the clients.

Some general points that can be highlighted when setting up a design and that need to be taken into account are as follows:

- Is my network adequately built for redundancy and will it be able to service all the different clients with the large amount of incoming data?
- Do I have enough storage to store my data and what will happen in case of a disk failure?
- Do my servers have enough compute performance to serve the number of clients available, or do I need to roll out more servers or invest in more hardware?
- Is my database solution scaled to handle the data flow? What happens if one of the database servers fails?
- What will happen if one of the servers in the site suffers a hardware failure?
- What happens if any other critical component in our infrastructure fails?

All these questions need to be taken into account and looked over, and taken into the planning phase. We always need to look over a design and think is there any single point of failure with this design? Because, it does not matter if we set up a massive and redundant SQL cluster in every way and we put the cluster on the same network switch. Because, then we know that if that particular switch goes down, the cluster goes down.

Coming back to Configuration Manager let us take a look at a simple site design for Configuration Manager and how it might look:

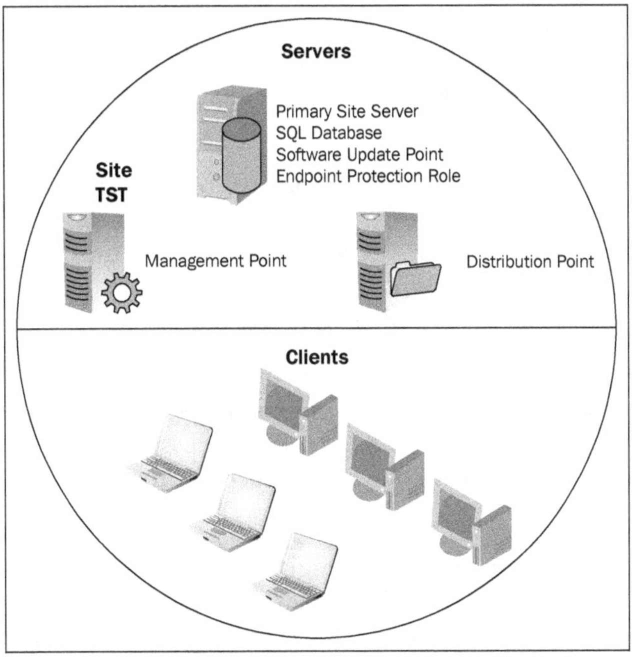

With a simple design shown in the previous diagram we have the general feature set for Configuration Manager available to our clients. All our Configuration Manager **Clients** will contact the **Management point** for policies, advertisements and reporting of data, and so on. The Management point in return will populate the site database with information received from the clients.

When the clients need to download a source file from an advertised deployment or for an operating system deployment it will contact the Distribution point within the site. For this site the data is stored in a single database server, which is collocated with the **Primary Site Server**. This design also includes a **Software Update Point** role as well as **Endpoint Protection Role** for the management of endpoint protection and patch management.

Let us look into problems with this type of design. For instance, let us see what would happen if the Management point server in the site stops functioning:

1. The clients will try to contact the Management point to get info about policy updates or report in data.
2. Since the Management point is unavailable, the clients will look at the list of available Management points in the site to see if there are any others available.

3. Since this site contains only one Management point, it will stop sending data back to the site and will start to cache the data locally and run using the last known configuration.
4. The clients will do so until the Management point is back online.

Let us see what would happen if we had two Management points in the site we just saw.

The clients would try to contact its first Management point; if it is offline it would look at its list of available Management points and try to contact the other one. This way we would have maintained site functionality for the clients. This gives us a Highly Available Management point solution for the clients, but this is only one of the components that need to be taken into account.

If the database stops working or suffers from a faulty hard drive at the server site, it would reflect outcomes that appear in the upcoming sections. As I mentioned earlier, clients will cache data locally until the site server is restored, but historical data will be lost. For instance, software metering information can be used for reporting licensing usage.

These were just a few examples of what might go wrong with this design. It is important to stay ahead when planning. There are also other components besides the ones we just covered in my example that need to be taken into account and they will be covered later in the book.

Networking

Does my core network have redundant paths to my switches? So in case a switch goes offline my servers are still available on network. Same goes for NIC teaming on the physical hosts.

Hardware

A solution such as RAID allows redundancy in case of a disk failure on physical servers, and depending on the RAID level, it might boost the server's performance. If you are unaware of what RAID does, we will go through this in greater detail later in the chapter.

Database server

Configuration Manager is highly dependent on a Microsoft SQL Server to store site data and client data. Microsoft has many built-in solutions for High Availability and they will be covered in a later chapter.

Virtualization hosts

Depending on where you want (either physical or virtual) to deploy Configuration Manager, you need to make sure that you have a Highly Available virtualization solution on the underlying hosts.

Other Configuration Manager roles

There are multiple roles in Configuration Manager that can be deployed as Highly Available, which are mandatory for most of the features (I will come back on this subject in a later chapter).

Backup

In case there are roles that cannot be set as highly available, what options do we have to back up the data and the role information, and how can we restore the service it offers to the users as quickly as possible?

Other components

Configuration Manager is highly dependent on other components such as DNS and Active Directory, and also Active Directory Certificate Services and DHCP. Are there any High Availability options for them? I will cover this topic more in detail in a later chapter.

But many of these roles are not a part of the design phase for a Configuration Manager solution, and in most cases are already set-up redundant. Further on in the upcoming chapters we will discuss how we can deploy each role and back-end services like Microsoft SQL Server using High Availability and load-balancing features, SQL Server. It is important to note that there are no services in Configuration Manager that happen in real time and that no clients require continuous communication with any of the site roles.

Configuration Manager always works on a predefined schedule for each operation; therefore you must expect some latency even if you set up High Availability for your sites.

Before we continue, we will take a look at how Microsoft IT deployed Configuration Manager for the environment, just to give a clearer image on how a large enterprise Configuration Manager deployment might look for a business. The following diagram gives its overview design:

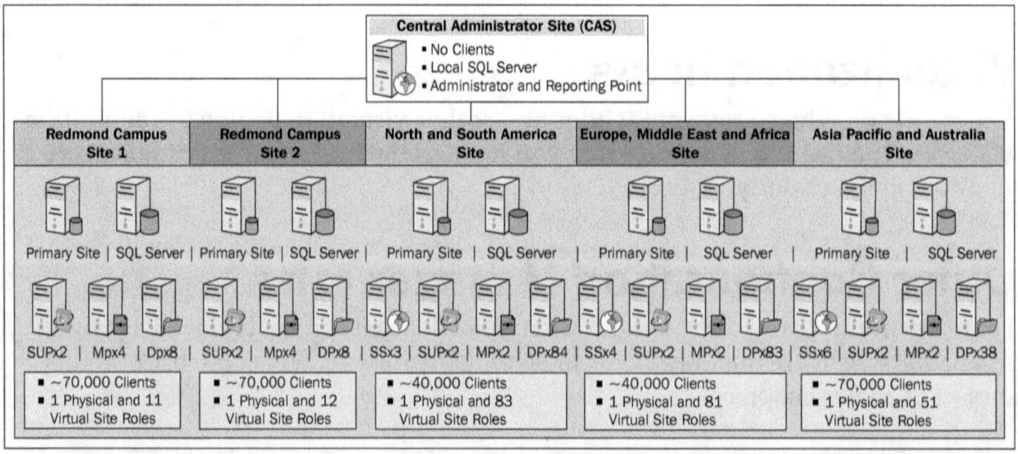

Microsoft IT deployed Configuration Manager 2012 for more than 250,000 systems and more than 150,000 users worldwide. Using this design and much of the logic that they use when deploying should be used in other scenarios as well as when planning.

The entire project can be found at the following site:

`http://www.microsoft.com/en-us/download/confirmation.aspx?id=29433`

A point to note here is that there are only six physical servers in the entire design. They are used on the site server roles, which have SQL Server installed (In this case, there is one each in the different Primary Sites and the CAS server).

> At the time Microsoft IT implemented Configuration Manager, Windows Server 2012 was not available and therefore, they chose not to virtualize the database servers in this design because of the hardware requirements for CPU.

Database planning

All of the servers which have Microsoft SQL Server installed are set up with different forms of RAID in order to gain redundancy and performance. This is needed because all the clients report back a large amount of data to the site, depending on what features are enabled in the client policy.

For instance, some examples of what the clients might report back to the site and the database are as follows:

- Software inventory
- Hardware inventory
- Software metering
- Baselines and configuration items

And depending on the information and the schedule this might result in a large amount of data.

But let us delve into the different forms of RAID and how it can give us better performance and redundancy for our database server. The whole purpose of RAID is to group together physical disks into a group and then form virtual disks on top to gain performance and redundancy. Now, there are different levels of RAID that we can setup

RAID 1 is a solution based on two disks where data is mirrored on both disks (so in case of a disk failure the service will continue to run on the other disk) when you replace the faulty disk the RAID controller will rebuild the data on the new disk until both disks have the same content again. This type of RAID will in theory give us 2x the read performance since the data is available on both disk, but this is very dependent on having an adequate RAID controller.

RAID 5 is a solution based on minimum three disks and it uses parity bits on each disk. Here data is split up in different chunks where two of the disks contains the data and the third disk contains the summary of the data on the other disks (known as a parity bit) For instance, if disk one contains the data bit, 1, and disk two contains the data bit, 1, then the parity disk would contain the data, 2. Since, it will always contain the sum of the different data from the other disks. If disk 1 should fail, it would take the parity and extract the data on disk 2, which will add up to 2 - 1 = 1. So it knows that the bits that are missing on the faulty disk is 1. Depending on the data the parity might be on different disks, so we do not use a dedicated disk for parity.

RAID 1+0 (or 10) is a combination of RAID levels 1 and 0 which does mirroring and splitting the data. All disks are members of two groups, where one group does the mirroring and the other group is for splitting the data. This can, in theory, give us 4x read and 2x write performance gain and redundancy in case of a disk failure and depending on the disks that fails, it can allow for two disks to fail.

> If you are unable to use RAID there is an alternative within Windows Server 2012, called Storage Spaces. This feature is set to be supported in SQL Server 2014. Support for SQL Server 2014 will come with Configuration Manager 2012 R2.

When Microsoft IT set up the CAS SQL Server, they used different levels of RAID depending on the purpose of the volume.

So let us take a better look on Microsoft setup and the layout of their database server. To explain in detail how Microsoft set up their database servers, have a look at the following volumes:

- **Volume C:**: This contains the OS setup with RAID 1)
- **Volume H:**: This contains the SQL Databases setup with RAID 1+0)
- **Volume D:**: This contains the SQL Database logs setup with RAID 1+0)
- **Volume E:**: This contains the backups setup with RAID 5)
- **Volume T:**: This contains SQL Database TempDB, which is setup with RAID 5)
- **Volume I:**: This contains the Configuration Manager files and is setup with RAID 1+0
- **Volume F:**: This contains the `Page` file and the WSUS updates that is setup with RAID 1

Some factors that are worth taking note are that they split the database setup so that they place the transaction logs on one volume, TempDB on one, and the regular databases on another one. With this type of setup you get better performance on the database service because of the way the different components and SQL work.

The TempDB database is responsible for storing all the temporary tables, temporary stored procedures, and internal objects created by the database engine. So any procedure in Configuration Manager that you use to create a temporary table will be stored in the TempDB.

The transaction logs store all the data transactions and database modifications. After these transactions are stored they are truncated to the database. These logs files will grow in size until a full backup has been done. This requires a lot of write activity and by placing them on a RAID 1+0 solution, we will have adequate performance.

It is also a best practice to store the swap file on a disk other than the regular OS disk. This will also boost our performance, since the swap file does not need to share IO with the regular system services. The other SQL Server on the primary sites are set up in an equal way as the CAS SQL to ensure that performance is not an issue for the large amounts of data.

It is important to note that you do not need to split up your database servers like this unless you require the extra performance and redundancy. But this type of deployment is according to best practice and should be used when possible, since Configuration Manager relies heavily on its database server.

We can also see in the design that Microsoft IT decided to use Secondary Sites in some of their regions. This is mostly because of the geographical gap between different countries. With Secondary Sites you can control the flow of data going back and forth between the sites.

Since secondary sites install a Management point and a Distribution point automatically, clients have what they need to get policy updates and content. As we can see from the site design, Microsoft uses a simple design for their solution. To sum up, following bullet points show how they deploy their service:

- Use CAS on the top of the hierarchy because of the large amount of clients, less than 400,000 clients
- Microsoft split up large geographical regions (Europe, Asia, and so on) as their own Primary sites
- Use secondary sites within primary sites to control the flow of data
- Multiple instances of each role within each site are used to have multiple instances available to the clients

Now, let's take a look into the different roles within Configuration Manager and see what kind of features they give and what they support. This will give you a better understanding on how you should scale and where you should use the different roles and components.

Central Administration site

Central Administrator site is the role that sits on top of the hierarchy (It is not mandatory but if you need more than one primary site you need this role to manage the different subprimary sites).

The features it contains are as follows:

- It can be installed along with the database server
- It cannot have any clients directly assigned to it
- It does processing of data from all the other primary sites in the hierarchy
- It can manage all the clients in the hierarchy
- It supports only Primary Sites as child sites

This site does not support all the different roles. For instance, it does support Endpoint Protection, Asset Intelligence, Reporting Services, Software Update point, Intune Connector, and System Health Validator point and some of these roles should be placed in top of the hierarchy.

This site supports the following:

- It can support up to 25 child primary sites
- When using SQL Datacenter or Enterprise it support up to 400,000 clients
- When using SQL Standard it supports up to 50,000 clients

> Before Service Pack 1, you would need to install CAS first when you were going to set up your hierarchy with multiple primary sites. This has changed after Service Pack 1. You can now add CAS to an existing Primary Site to extend your hierarchy.

Primary sites

It is the most commonly-deployed site method and is a mandatory role when deploying Configuration Manager.

Now a primary site can have the following features:

- It can be standalone or part of a hierarchy either with a CAS and other Primary site or a Primary with subsecondary sites
- It is responsible for processing all data from its assigned clients
- It uses database replication to communicate with its CAS
- It can be installed with the database server
- It can have clients assigned to it

The primary site has support for the following:

- It can have up to 250 Secondary sites in its hierarchy
- It can manage up to 100,000 clients
- It can manage up to 10,000 Windows Embedded clients
- When having a SQL Server collocated with the site server it can have up to 50,000 clients
- A standalone primary site supports all the different roles. When a primary site is part of a bigger hierarchy, it no longer support having Asset Intelligence point, Endpoint Protection, or Synchronization point installed

- It can have up to 10 Management points connected
- Also, it can have up to 250 Distribution points connected

Secondary sites

This can only be set up as a child site to another primary site and participates in file-based replication to communicate with its parent Primary Site. This is not a mandatory role and should only be considered if you want to control the transmission of client data up the hierarchy. However, secondary sites do not have all the functionality of a primary site and must be a child site of an existing primary site.

A secondary site has the following features:

- It is installed with an SQL Express automatically if a SQL instance is not installed previously
- Installs a Management point and Distribution point on the same server
- Software Update point and State Migration point can also be installed
- Sends data to its primary site using file-based replication

Also, it can support the following:

- It can have only one Management point
- It can have up to 250 Distribution points
- It can manage up to 5,000 clients

It is important to note that Microsoft recommends that we try to avoid using secondary sites whenever possible, and just work with a regular primary site and use the different features which are included with the Distribution point. This will be covered in the next chapter.

Management point

A Management point has the following features:

- Primary contact point for clients within a site is present. You can also install a Management with a connection to a Site Replica database to reduce CPU cycles on the Site database server.
- Clients have to be connected to a Management point to communicate with a site.
- It can support having up to 25,000 clients.

If you have a remote location (for instance, on a low bandwidth WAN) you should not configure a Management point at the remote location. This is because a Management point is not aware of the site, unlike a Distribution point, which you can place within a boundary. If you place a Management point at the remote location, clients from another part of the site might actually use that Management point and cause more traffic on the WAN link. In this case, it would be better suited to use a secondary site.

Distribution point

The Distribution point is responsible for delivering data to the clients, both for applications and OS deployment and also, it has the following features:

- It allows streaming of applications using App-V
- It allows PXE connections using unicast or multicast
- It allows rate limiting and pull-based content deployment.
- It supports up to 4,000 clients
- It supports a combined total up to 10,000 applications and packages

Software Update point

Software Update point is integrated with Windows Server Update Services (WSUS) to deliver software updates to clients using Configuration Manager.

WSUS can be deployed on a regular Windows Server with either using a Windows Internal Database or using a regular Microsoft SQL Server. It supports the following features:

- It supports up to 25,000 clients (when installed with the site server)
- It supports up to 100,000 clients (when installed on another server that is not the site server)

Before Service Pack 1, you were restricted to having only one Software Update point in each site. Now with Service Pack 1, you can install multiple Software Update roles within a site.

Fallback Status point

The Fallback point allows clients to send status messages back to the site in case there is trouble with locating its Management point or for instance, trouble connecting to the site.

It is also useful if we want to use the client deployment report, which displays data received from the Fallback Status point. It is important to note that this role runs on regular HTTP and therefore it's not encrypted. This role supports up to 100,000 users and should be on a dedicated server.

Application Catalog Website point & Web Service point

These roles allow users to access a self-service portal for applications that are published to them. The portal itself is based solely upon Silverlight, both of these roles support up to 50,000 clients each.

Reporting Services point

The reporting role is attached to a SQL reporting instance to generate Configuration Manager Reports from the console.

This role copies over Configuration Manager Reports and applies security policies based upon the security settings in the site. It is important to note that only one reporting role can be attached to a SQL reporting instance.

There are other roles that can also be a part of the installation, which I'm not going to cover in detail in this chapter, but the following points might be worth looking into:

- State Migration point
- System Health Validator point
- Intune point
- Enrollment point
- Enrollment Proxy point
- Asset Intelligence synchronization point

More information about these roles can be found on Microsoft technet at

`http://technet.microsoft.com/en-us/library/hh272770.aspx`.

But there are some components that are important and are required for most of the roles in Configuration Manager. They are as follows:

- **Internet Information Services (IIS)**: This is a web server role, which is included in Windows Server. The majority of the roles in Configuration Manager require having this role installed, since it allows clients to communicate with the server using HTTP or HTTPS.

- **Background Intelligent Transfer Service** (**BITS**): This is a component, which is included in most of the operating systems from Microsoft. It allows asynchronous, prioritized, and throttled transfer of files between machines using available network bandwidth. BITS is used by Configuration Manager to deliver content to the clients.
- **Remote Differencial Compression** (**RDC**): This is an algorithm, which is used to analyze a situation where a file exists on two computers and that file is modified. Only the differing sectors need to be sent to the other computer. Site Servers and Distribution points use this to generate package signatures. So when we update a package it will only send over those sectors that have changed.

Network flow

In a moment, you will see how the different roles and clients communicate with each other. This information will be useful when setting up or planning firewall rules between servers and clients, and roles that can be load balanced.

Network communication flow is described in the following table:

Description	Protocol	Client/Server	Ports
Client DHCP to PXE point	UDP	Distribution point with PXE	67, 68 69 (TFTP)
Client to Distribution point	TCP	Distribution point	80 or 443
Client to Fallback Status point	TCP	Fallback Status point	80
Client to Management point	TCP	Management point	80 or 443, 10123(Client Notification)
Client to Software Update Point	TCP	Software Update point	80 & 8530 or 443 & 8531
Client to Cloud Distribution point	TCP	Azure Distribution point	443
Client to State Migration point	TCP	State Migration point	80 or 443 and 445
Client to Application catalog	TCP	Application catalog	80 or 443
Client to Global Catalog Domain Controller	TCP	Domain Controller I Active Directory	3268 or 3269

Description	Protocol	Client/Server	Ports
Configuration Manager Console to Client (Remote tools)	TCP	Clients	2701 for Remote Control and 3389 for Remote Assistance
Management point to Site Server	TCP	Management point to Site Server	135, 445 and Dynamic ports in RCP range
Management point to Global Catalog Domain Controller	TCP	Active Directory	3268 or 3269, 135, 445 and Dynamic ports in RCP range
Management point to SQL Server	TCP	SQL Server	1433
Site Server to SQL Server	TCP	SQL Server	1433
SQL Server to SQL Server	TCP	SQL Server	1433 and 4022 SQL Service Broker
Application Catalog Web Service point to SQL Server	TCP	SQL Server	1433
Application Catalog Website point to Application Catalog Service point	TCP	Catalog website to Catalog Service point	80 or 443
Site Server to server roles	TCP/UDP	Site Server connects to another server role	445 (TCP) 135 (TCP/UDP) and Dynamic Ports in RPC range
Software Update point to Internet	TCP	Software Update point to connect to Microsoft	80
Software Update point to Upstream WSUS Server	TCP	Software Update point to internal WSUS server	80 and 8530 or 443 and 8531
Exchange Server Connector to Exchange Online	TCP	Site Server to Exchange Online, for instance, Office365	5986
Exchange Server Connector to Exchange on premise	TCP	Site Server to Exchange server	5985

Some important factors regarding port usage within Configuration Manager are as follows:

- Most of the traffic is either based upon HTTP (port 80) or HTTPS (port 443) depending on whether you have deployed a PKI infrastructure or not.
- Some roles require the use of port 445 based on SMB traffic (regular file transfer protocol).
- Some roles also require the use of a dynamic range of ports from the RPC protocol. The range for RPC is between port 49152 and 65535.
- RPC also uses port 135.
- Most SQL connections use port 1433, which is the standard SQL port for SQL to SQL connections. SQL also use port 4022, which is used by the SQL function service broker, which is used to replicate between parent and child SQL Server.
- Different client installation methods use different ports, where manual installation can use either HTTP/HTTPS 80 or 443 and SMB 445. Client push installation uses a combination of the previous ports and dynamic RPC ones.

New in Service Pack 1

Before we continue on how to deploy High Availability, it is import to note some of the changes that have been done to the Service Pack 1 release. Some of the new features are large hierarchy changes that can affect the site design. It has the following features:

- Support to update client notifications from the Console
- Support for Windows Server 2012 for Site Systems and clients
- Support for Microsoft SQL Server 2012 for Site databases
- Support to place a Distribution point in Windows Azure
- Support for multiple Service Update points within a site
- Support to expand a primary site into a hierarchy including a CAS
- Support for PowerShell
- Support for pull-based Distribution points
- Support for agents on Mac clients, Linux servers, and UNIX servers
- Support to configure users' profile settings such as folder redirection, offline files, and roaming profiles

- Support for applications that has been created using Microsoft Application Virtualization Version 5.0
- Support for thin clients using Windows Embedded
- Support for endpoint protection for Mac clients, Linux servers and UNIX servers
- Support for Intune integration for mobile device management

> During the writing of this book, System Center 2012 R2 is in the making and is expected to be released October 18, 2013, the release will focus more on Intune and mobile device management.
>
> Also it will support the next wave of operating systems Windows 8.1 and Windows Server 2012 R2.

Summary

In this chapter, we have gone through the different components and roles within Configuration Manager, what their functions are, and how they scale. We looked into different components which need to be taken into account when planning for High Availability such as networking, hardware, and other critical infrastructure components such as AD, DNS, and DHCP.

We also took a closer look at how Microsoft IT has deployed their Configuration Manager solution to get a better overview on how a site design with High Availability might look like.

In the next chapter, we will start by going through how we can set up the different roles and features to become highly available.

2

Configuring Roles for High Availability

Now it's down to the real deal—the bits and bytes. In this chapter, we will go through different roles and services and how they can be deployed as highly available for the clients. We will also walk through some examples of how a simple site design might look like for different scenarios. So, the topics we will go through in this chapter are:

- How to set up high-availability roles and features within Configuration Manager
- Different ways to perform content distribution
- Client communication and behavior
- Example site designs

First, let's take a look at roles within Configuration Manager that cannot be deployed as highly available and what options we have.

It is important to note that when installing a site system role on another server Configuration Manager, the installation files are installed on the first available NTFS disk with maximum available disk space. If you wish to exclude a disk, create an empty file called `no_sms_on_drive.sms` on the root folder of the drive. Also, Configuration Manager uses the site server computer account to try to install the role on a remote server (so, this account needs to be added to local administrator on the server) unless we specify a domain account (which also needs to be a local admin) when we run the setup.

Site Server

The first and foremost important role that cannot be deployed as highly available is the Site Server role. It does not support network load balancing or other clustering features available in Windows Server. In order to make sure that you can restore the site in case of disaster, you have to use the built-in backup tasks. I will cover this in more detail in a later chapter.

Endpoint Protection

The **Endpoint Protection** role allows for management of endpoint protection agents.

If this role is unavailable for the clients, they will still continue to run as before but you cannot update the policy centrally. This role is not seen as critical for Configuration Manager and cannot be deployed as highly available. If something happens to your endpoint server, just reinstall the role on another server. It is important to know that this role can only be deployed once at the top of your hierarchy; so, if we have a CAS, we would place this role there. Same is true if we have a standalone primary site with secondary sites.

Asset Intelligence Synchronization Point

The **Asset Intelligence Synchronization Point** role connects to System Center online (a cloud service from Microsoft) in order to update the asset catalog with the latest information. If this role becomes unavailable, the site will just store data locally until it becomes online and is able to synchronize again. This role cannot be deployed as highly available, and it is important to note that this role can only be installed on the CAS role (if present) or on a standalone primary site as well.

Fallback Status Point

The **Fallback Status Point** role is used to monitor client deployments and the clients that are unable to connect to their management point, or if there is something wrong with the management point. All communication between clients and this role happens over regular HTTP requests and therefore this role should be placed on a standalone server.

> All status messages that get sent to the Fallback Status Point role will be registered in the logfiles `fspisapi.log` and `fspmgr.log`.

This role is not considered critical and cannot be deployed as highly available.

It is important to note that clients can only be assigned to one fallback point and the assignment happens during client installation.

Out of Band Service Point

The **Out of Band Service Point** role is used to manage and provision clients which have Intel vPRO or Intel AMT functionality, which allows Configuration Manager to manage clients before the operating system is active.

This role cannot be deployed as highly available.

Secondary sites

Secondary sites by default contain one distribution point and one management point, and as mentioned previously, should only be used when you need control on how data is moved up the hierarchy.

A secondary site does not support more than one management point. Data for a secondary site is primarily located in the primary site database. You can recover a secondary site by reinstalling it from its primary site.

Windows Intune Connector

The **Windows Intune Connector** role is a new role with Service Pack 1. It allows for mobile management from Configuration Manager using Windows Intune. This role can only be installed once and it needs to be in the top-level site in the hierarchy.

So, now that we have covered the roles that cannot be deployed as highly available, let us go forward with the roles that we can deploy as highly available.

Management Point

The **Management Point** role is used by clients for policy downloads, data reporting, and is the primary role for client-to-site communication.

When a client is assigned to a site (depending on how you have defined the client installation parameters), it will download a list of all the available management points in the site and get assigned to an appropriate one. The clients will connect to another management point if one of the following happens:

- Client restarts
- Network changes

- 25 hours have passed
- The contact with its primary management point is lost

It will also check if the management point is Intranet-only or is available from the Internet, and if it communicates using HTTP or HTTPS. (Remember that if the management point is set up on the Internet, only HTTPS traffic is allowed.)

Now besides manual installation, clients will look for a management point within one of the following locations if something from one of the points mentioned above happens:

> When installing a client manually, you can append the parameters `CCMSetup.exe /mp:MPFQDN SMSSITECODE=SITECODE FSP=FSPFQDN.` to define which management point to contact, which site to register to, and which FSP to contact.

- **Site information:** After a client has successfully signed up with a site, it will download a list of available management points which it stores in its cache. If it does not have any other management point available, it will continue looking in other locations.
- **Active Directory**: This only applies if you have extended the schema. Configuration Manager can publish management points directly under System Management Container with the site code. (This can be disabled under **Administration** | **Sites** | **Site Properties** | **Configure Site Components** | **Management Point**.)

> Extending the schema expands the Active Directory schema with specific Configuration Manager attributes. This allows clients to locate specific Configuration Manager server roles such as Management Points, boundaries, and its site from Active Directory. This is an irreversible action, but it allows for clients to easily locate site resources.

The site code and the management points that are available within the site will be stored under **Active Directory Users and Computer** | **Domain** | **System** | **System Management**. As you can see in the following screenshot, the clients will look here if there is another management point available within this container:

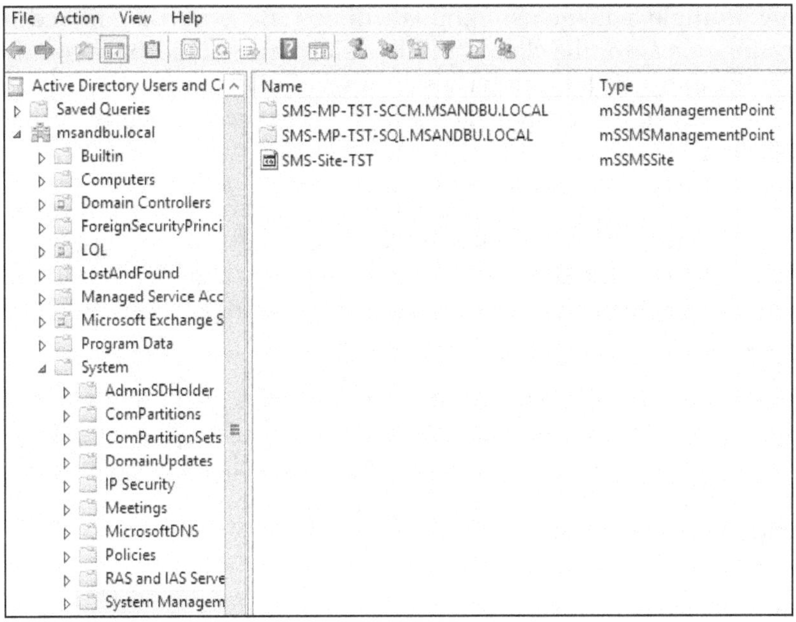

- **DNS**: Clients will write a DNS query for service locator point record within the current domain. All management points will appear within the DNS zone as a prefix `_mssms_mp_SITECODE`, with a port number, and which host it is pointing to. These DNS records can also be automatically be published by Configuration Manager and can be disabled from the same location as Active Directory publishing. The following screenshot shows the **DNS** zone showing management point:

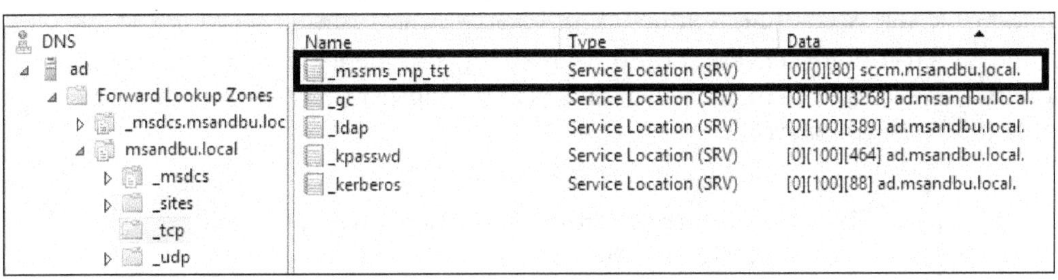

- **WINS**: If your organization is using WINS, Configuration Manager can also publish site information there as well.

If a client manages to find another management point within one of the locations mentioned in the preceding list, it will try to establish a connection with it.

By installing multiple management points within a site, you will gain redundant communication points for the clients within a site. Since clients have multiple places to get the information, you have multiple fallback points. There is no extra configuration required for the management points to become highly available after they are installed.

It is also important to note that by default the management point talks directly to the site database server, to query for data and to publish data. If we want to reduce the CPU processing against the site database, we can set up a management point against a SQL replica. This requires that we set up a site server database with the same SQL replication installed for the site replica database.

When we set up this management point, we will always query the replica database for information, but since the replication happens one-way (site to replica) the management point will always need to contact the site database to write data to the site. But we can set up multiple management points to talk to the SQL replica server, this will help to offload the site-server database.

Distribution point

Distribution points plays the vital role of delivering content to the clients.

Whenever a client needs to download a new operating system or just the bits of an application or a package, it needs to contact a distribution point on the site. It is important to note how a client locates its distribution point, this is done by creating boundaries.

In Configuration Manager 2012, we have to define a boundary or multiple boundaries and place them within a boundary group. Within these groups we define which content servers should be available for clients within the boundaries. Boundaries are used to make the client select the closest server from which the content is to be transferred.

> Content servers are either distribution points or state migration servers.

Under the properties of the **Boundary Group -My Site Properties** page we can define which content servers are available for clients. Also, we can define it for a site assignment as shown in the following screenshot:

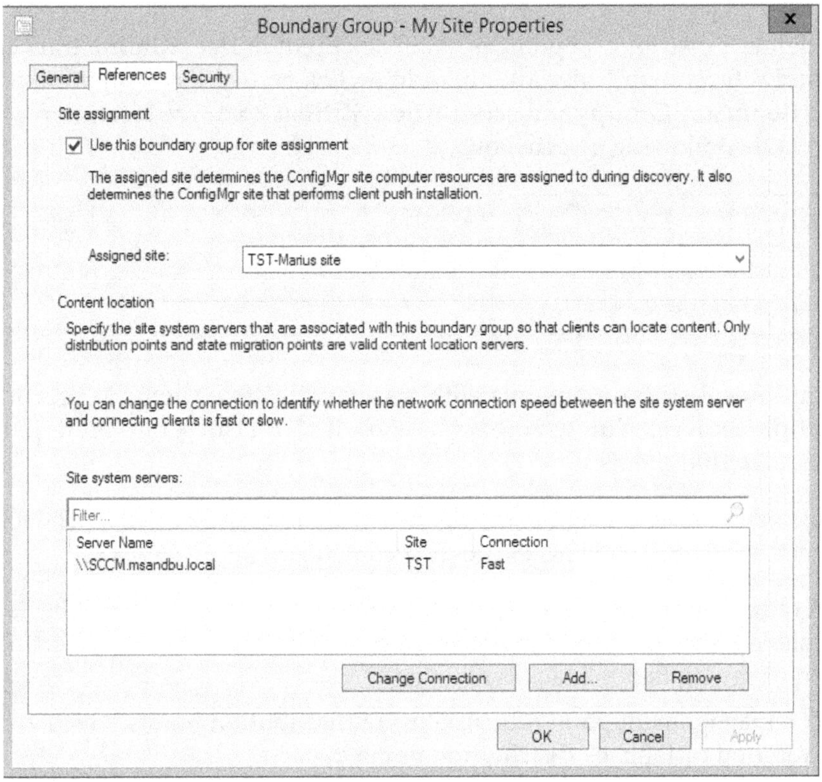

Boundaries can be created based upon the following:

- IP subnet
- Active Directory site name
- IPv6 prefix
- IP address range

> We can also configure the `Forest Discovery` function to automatically create boundaries for each IP subnet and Active Directory site it discovers.

For instance, if I have a branch office which has two subnets, I can create a boundary for each of the subnets and place them in a boundary group. This will place the clients from the two subnets within the same boundary group.

Now if a client is located within this boundary, it will always try to get the content from the preferred server here (`SCCM.MSANDBU.LOCAL` in my example). If this distribution point does not have the content, the client will try to locate a fallback distribution point which has the content if there is a defined one.

You can define a distribution point as a fallback point under **Administration | Servers and Site System Roles** and then right-click on the distribution point server and go to **Boundary Groups** and select **Allow Fallback Source location for content** as shown in the following screenshot:

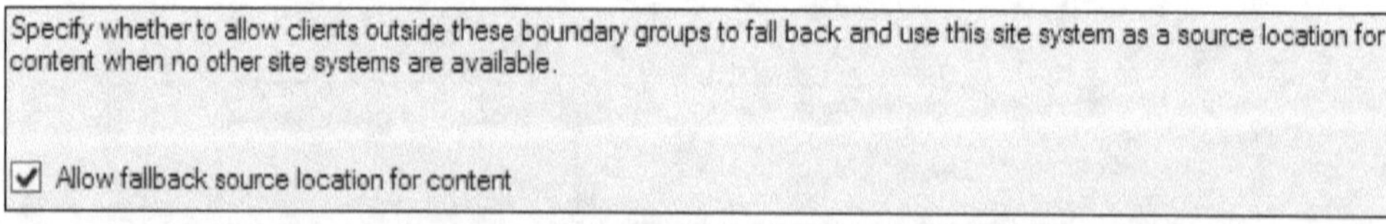

Having multiple distribution points within a site will allow clients to get content from multiple sources. With having set boundaries, you can set up preferred content servers for all of the clients.

It is important to understand how the clients try to locate their content. The following are the ways in which the clients locate their content:

- A client sends a content request to its management point (if fallback is enabled, the clients will mark the information that is sent to the management point saying that fallback is allowed)
- The management point returns a list of distribution points which are either preferred or fallback distribution points
- The clients will try to locate the content on the preferred distribution point; if the content is not there, it will try the fallback distribution point
- If the content is not available on either of them, the client will fail with an error message **Content is not available** and will make a new request every hour

PXE distribution point

for OS deployment PXE is crucial, but there is no high-availability options for PXE available. We can however set up multiple distribution points with PXE activated within the same subnets. In order to make sure that these points do not trip on each other we have to set up a start delay on the Distribution point. This way we can prioritize which distribution point should be used to boot from first.

You can set this delay on the PXE pane under the properties of the distribution point using the option **Specify the PXE server response delay**.

Cloud-based distribution point

Cloud distribution point is a cloud-based content service which is hosted on Windows Azure and is not like a regular distribution point. Although it can deliver content to clients, it has the following limitations:

- You cannot use a cloud-based distribution point to host software updates
- You cannot use a cloud-based distribution point for PXE or multicast deployments
- You cannot use a cloud-based distribution point during a task sequence that requires a task to download content locally when needed by running task sequence
- You cannot use a cloud-based distribution point to offer packages that are set up with run from distribution point
- You cannot use a cloud-based distribution point to host virtualized applications

However, you can manage the cloud-based distribution point like a regular distribution point, individually or as a part of the distribution group. If you need more instances of cloud based distribution points, you can scale up within Windows Azure since it is a regular storage blob.

It is also important to note that content that is sent from Configuration Manager to Azure is encrypted before it is sent.

In order to allow clients to communicate with a cloud-based distribution point, you must allow access under **Cloud Services** within the **Client Policy** settings. Remember that you are charged by data transfer in Azure, so remember to set a threshold within Configuration Manager.

To set up a cloud-based distribution point, we have to use the **Create Cloud Distribution Point in the Cloud** node under **Hierarchy Configurations**. This requires an active Microsoft Azure subscription and a management certificate setup in Azure. Also, you need a digital-signed certificate with an FQDN which can be resolved via DNS by the clients which are going to use this distribution point.

> I'm not going to cover how to create a management certificate or how to create an Azure Account. The procedures to create both of these can be found at `www.windowsazure.com`. You can create a trial account in Azure if you wish to test this functionality.

If we want to create a cloud distribution point, we can right-click on **Administration** and then in the section under **Overview**, expand **Hierarchy Configuration** and select **Cloud** and then choose **Create Cloud Distribution Point**.

First we have to enter the subscription ID (which can be located in Azure) and then we have to add the management certificate. Configuration Manager needs this certificate in order to manage the account in Azure.

Next we have to define multiple settings. First we have to define where we want this service located. Azure has multiple data centers around the world, which again is split up in regions, as you can see in the following screenshot. The closer the service is to your location, the better bandwidth and latency you get.

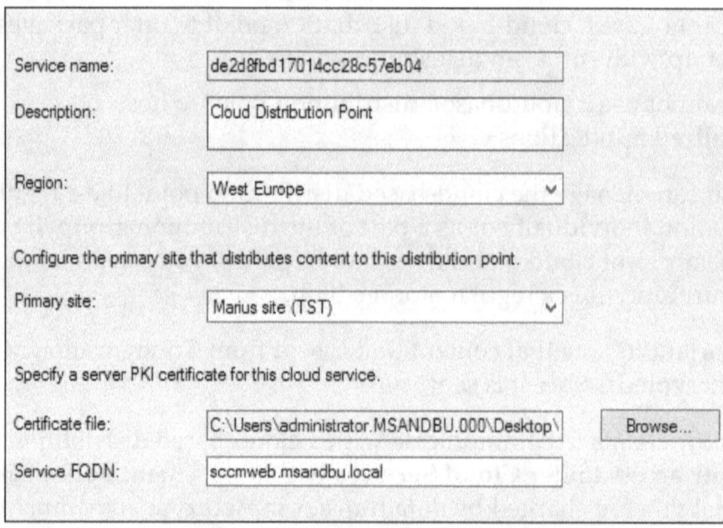

We also need to define which primary site should be associated with this point. We also need to add a certificate which we have created from our internal PKI service. The service name here needs to have a certificate which is trusted by your clients or else they will not connect to it.

Also, the FQDN here needs to be added to your DNS service pointing to the VIP address over the service.

Next, we need to configure thresholds for this service. When having a service running in Azure, we are being billed for compute hours, storage place, and bandwidth usage. So, in order to control the usage here, we can define alerts and thresholds in GB, as shown in the following screenshot:

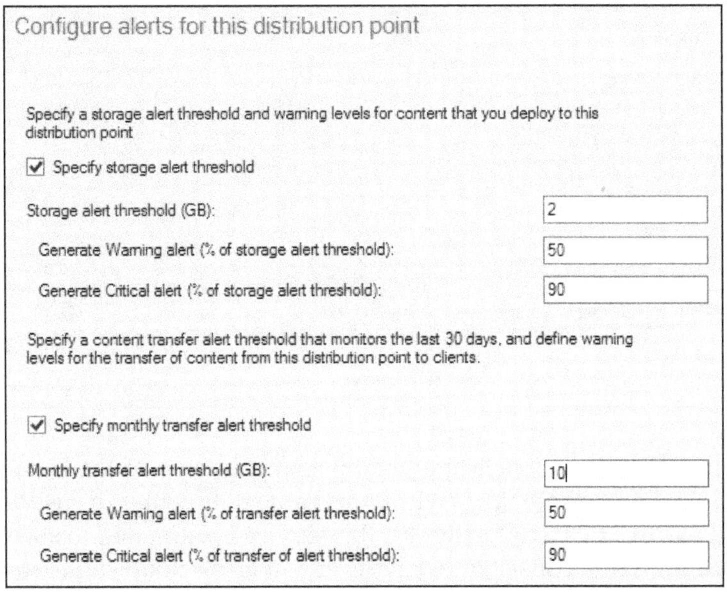

After we are finished with the setup of the cloud-based distribution point, we have to go into the clients policy settings and define that clients are allowed to use it, as shown in the following screenshot:

> You should only deploy these settings to clients who we want to use a cloud-based distribution point.

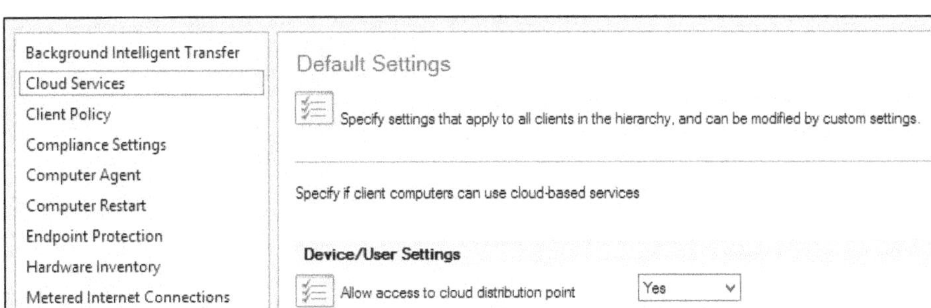

Now we can go into monitoring and see that the distribution point has finished provisioned and is ready to use:

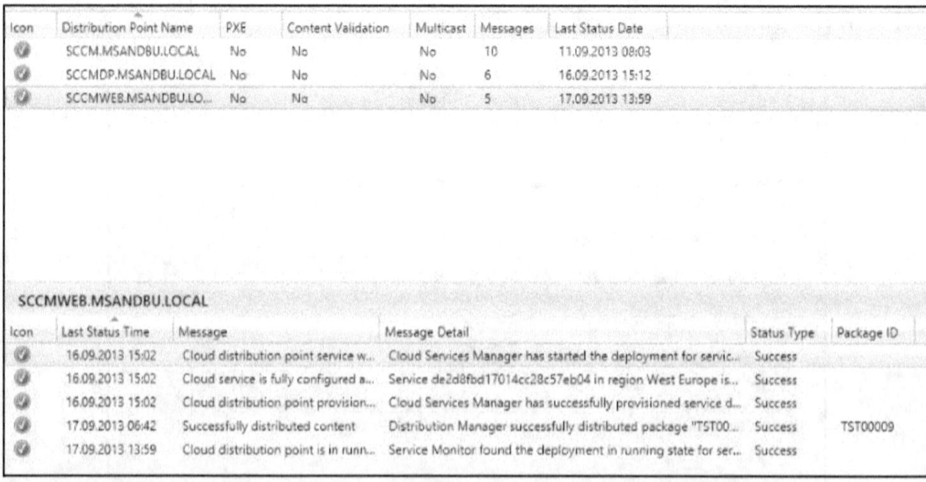

High availability for this service is handled by Azure automatically. Data is automatically replicated three times within the same data center to ensure redundancy, and Microsoft ensures that availability for this service is estimated to 99.99 percent. The service within Azure consist of two services—it is the cloud service and the storage containers. The cloud part is just a service running on top of virtual machines which are publically available via the **VIP** (**Virtual IP**) address. The virtual machines access the content within the storage containers. We can see the VIP address located under cloud services overview. This is the IP address (highlighted in the following screenshot) which needs to be added to your DNS zone:

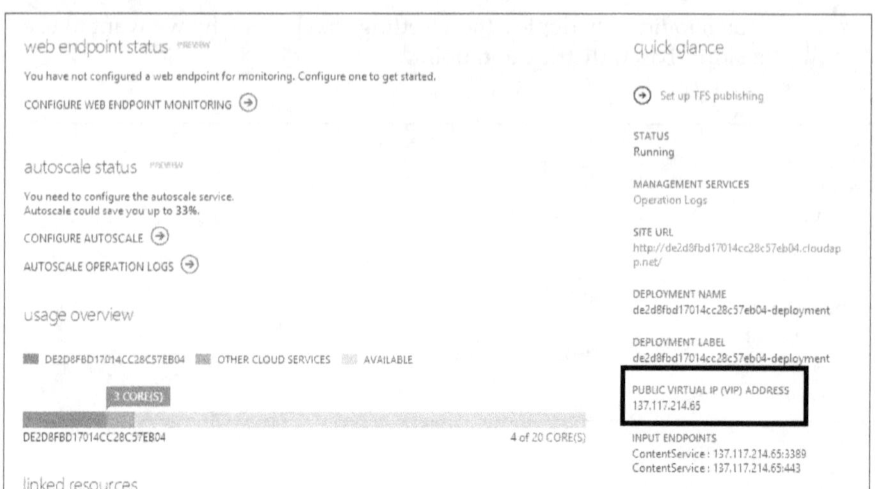

We can also see that when we distribute content from our primary site to the cloud-based point, it will automatically create a container for the package within the storage container:

By default this cloud service runs on top of two instances (virtual machines). We can adjust the number of instances accessible to the cloud service to ensure enough performance; we can adjust the number of instances available to the service under the scale menu. It is important to note that adjusting this might affect the cost of the azure subscription.

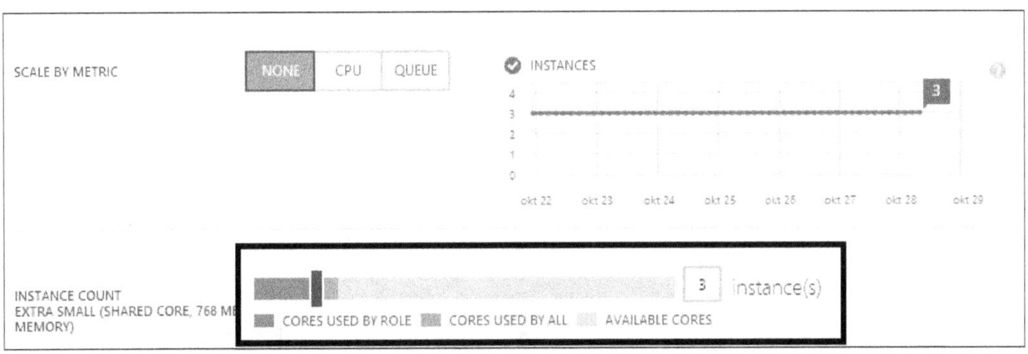

Even if we adjust the scale here,. we will still have one distribution point available to the clients within this region. We can add multiple distribution points if we wish.

Pull-based distribution point

This is a new feature which came with Service Pack 1, which allows offloading of the content distribution from the site server itself.

With pull-based distribution, you can define a distribution point where other distribution servers are to get content from. Instead of distributing all the content from the site server (which places extra load on the site server), a pull-based distribution point will try to get content from another distribution point which is defined as a source distribution point.

This will make the content transfer more efficient since the site server does not need to distribute content to all the distribution points itself.

Also this can make content moving much more efficient because in a traditional content distribution, the site server has to move the content to the distribution point or the group.

> A cloud-based distribution point cannot be set up as a pull-based or as a source distribution point.

The following diagram shows a regular content deployment process:

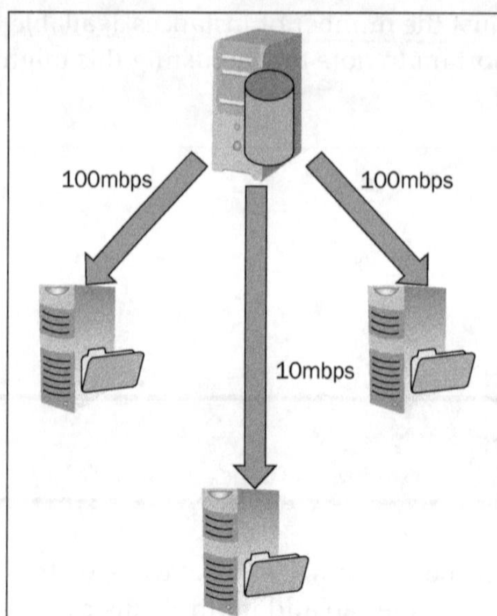

So in the preceding example, the site server has to move content to three different distribution points which are located on different locations. If we use pull-based distribution point on the location with the lowest bandwidth and one of the other as a source distribution point, content will move from site to a point and then to the other point.

The following diagram shows content deployment with a pull-based distribution from source distribution points:

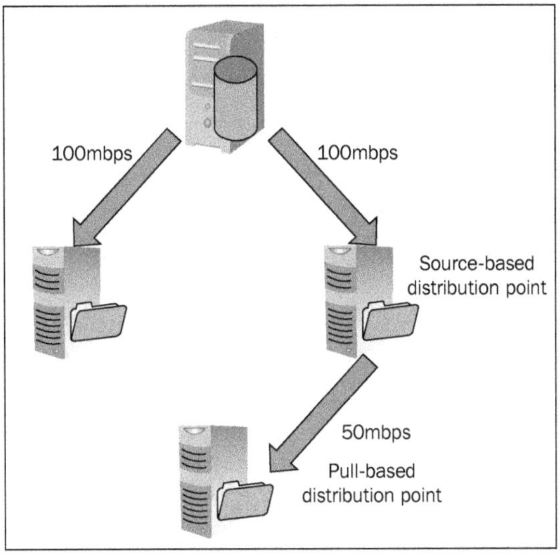

You can set this from within the properties of the distribution point and you also add what distribution points should be added as the source distribution point. You can set the pull-based distribution point by navigating to **Administration** | **Servers and Site system roles** | **Server** | **Distribution Point** | **Properties**. Then check **Enable this distribution point to pull content from other distribution points**, as shown in the following screenshot:

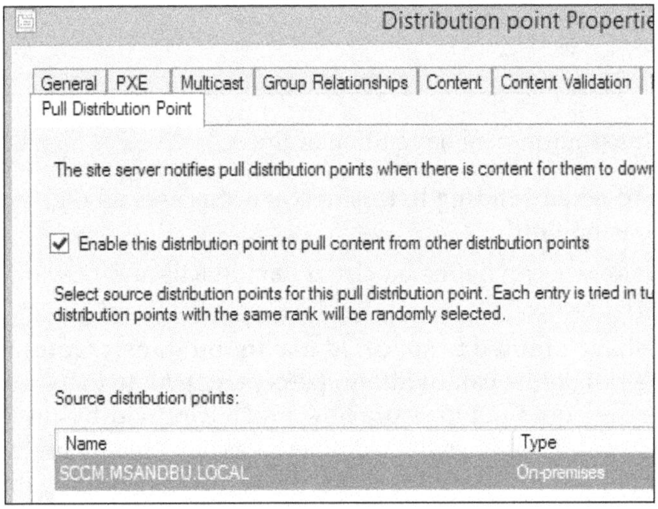

And if we have better bandwidth from one remote location to the other, this would make content moving more efficient and also remove unnecessary CPU usage from the site server.

It is also important to note that on distribution points we have the ability to define a rate limit for how much bandwidth we use to send content to the distribution point based on an hourly schedule.

Rate limiting options

The following screenshot shows the options in rate limiting:

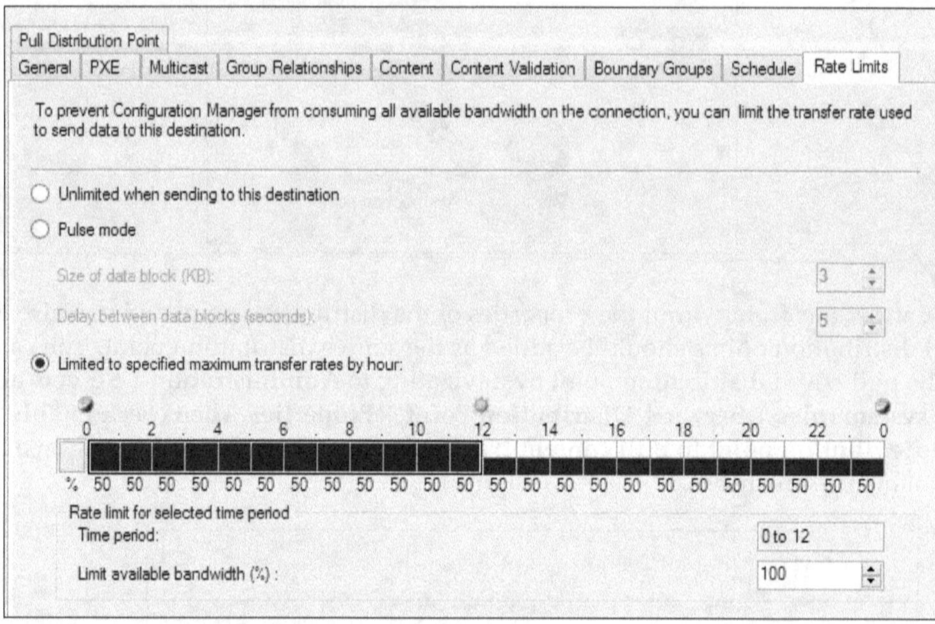

When defining rate limiting we have three options:

- **Unlimited when sending to this destination** (uses all the available bandwidth).
- **Pulse mode** (we can define blocks of data in KBs and how often we send these blocks).
- Then we have **Limited to specified maximum transfer rates by hour** (here, we can define bandwidth in percentage). Note that Configuration Manager here does not measure how much bandwidth is used. For instance, between 0 and 1 A.M. we have defined it as 50 percent bandwidth. It will send content for the first 30 minutes then stop transmitting for the next 30 minutes.

Distribution points are one of the most crucial components in a Configuration Manager solution, and we have multiple ways of deploying it depending on what is needed. We also have a lot of flexibility on how we can distribute content around the site with the use of either rate limiting or pull-based distribution points. We can also use cloud-based distribution points for Internet-based clients if we wish.

A site design for distribution will differ every time, but it is important to note what options we have.

Application Catalog Website point

The Application Catalog Website is the web portal that the users see when they want to access the software catalog. The portal itself runs a Silverlight XAP module which generates the software catalog based on the application that is deployed to the user.

In order to generate this data, the website point role has to communicate with the web service point, which in turn accesses the site database to get the information it needs.

When you install these roles, you can install them on multiple servers to ensure high availability, as when you set up the client's policy, you can define the computers to **Automatically detect** and they will be redirected to an available instance within the site.

This, however, has its weaknesses since you would require a certificate for each instance of this role we have set up, and we have no other option but to do round robin to different instances.

We could also set up multiple website points and use different client policies for different types of devices.

If you have the ability to set up this in a load-balanced solution (for instance, if you have a solution such as KEMP, Citrix Netscaler, or F5 BIG-IP), this would be most recommended.

To show you how this would look in a load-balanced solution, I did a quick setup of Citrix Netscaler VPX (Virtual Appliance) to show how you can load balance 2x Application Catalog Website point servers.

The websites themselves are using regular HTTP to communicate, but the load-balanced solution is using HTTPS. We have the load balancer do an SSL offload which removes CPU cycles from the web servers themselves.

> I will not walk through how to create a digital certificate which is crucial to having a successful setup of this website role; if you wish to try this yourself, you can download a trial version for Netscaler from Citrix `http://www.citrix.com/products/netscaler-application-delivery-controller/try.html`.

When setting up a load balancer, you always need to have two IP addresses for the service—one VIP (this is the IP address for the load-balanced service that users will connect to) and one SNIP (Subnet IP address, this is the IP address that will initiate contact with the backend service on behalf of the client).

To set up load balancing within Citrix Netscaler, do the following:

1. Add the servers that have the website role installed that you wish to load balance by navigating to **Traffic Management** | **Load Balancing** | **Servers**:

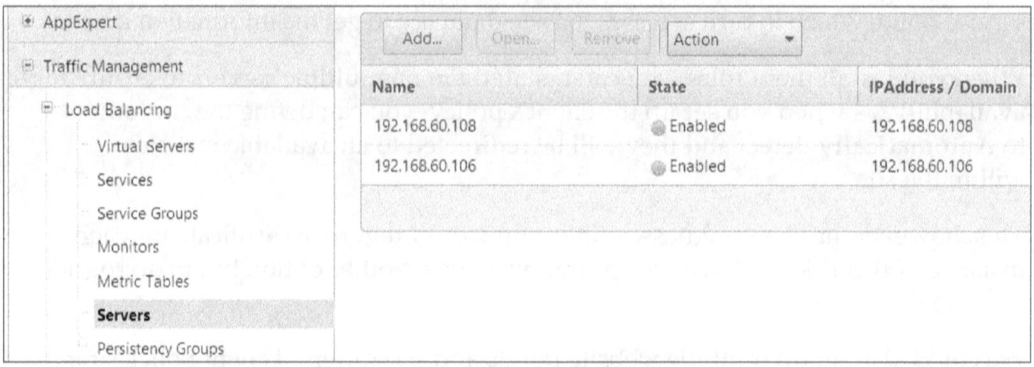

2. As shown in the following screenshot, add the kind of service on those two servers we wish to load balance. In this case, we have an HTTP service and we need to add a monitor which will be used from the Netscaler to the backend web server to see whether the server is available or not. (If a service does not reply to the monitor, Netscaler will take the server down from the load-balanced solution.)

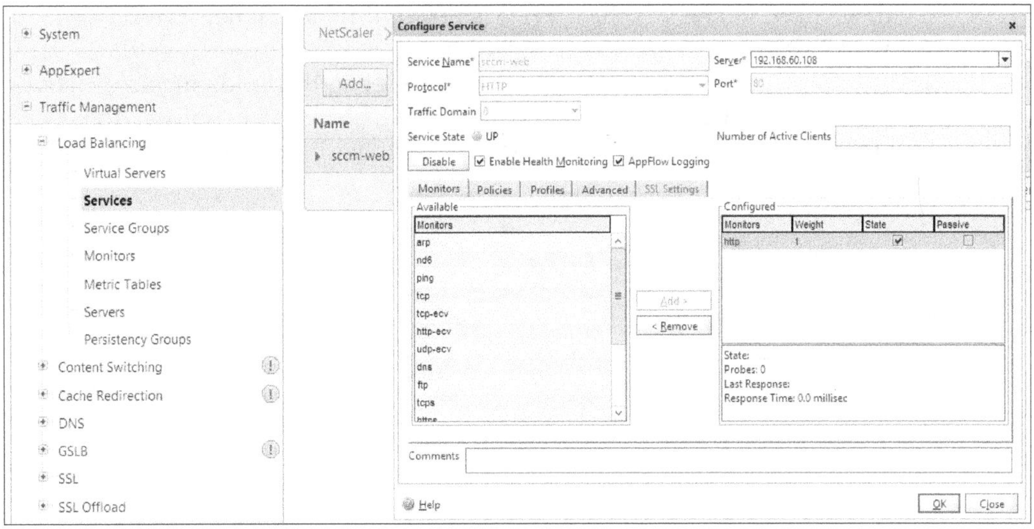

3. Next, we create the virtual service. Choose an IP address of the (VIP) service we created earlier and choose which type of protocol we want to use (in this case, it is HTTPS) and add a digital certificate in order to ensure that the communication is encrypted, as shown in the following screenshot:

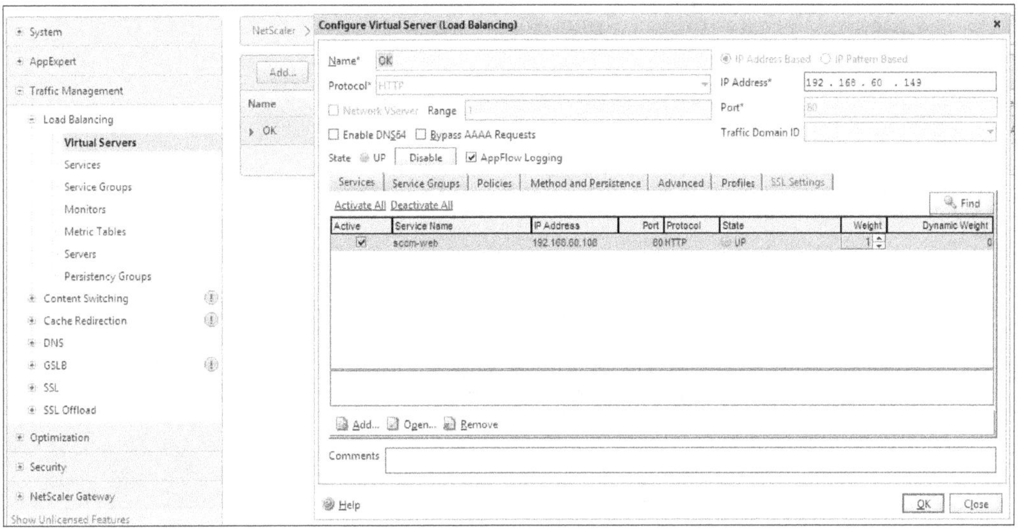

4. Next, we need to check if the service is responding to the new IP address using HTTPS. In my case, the new URL is `https://sccmweb.msandbu.local/CMapplicationCatalog/` as you can see in the following screenshot. And if we did not add a signed certificate to the Netscaler solution, the user will receive error messages from the browser about the site not being trusted.

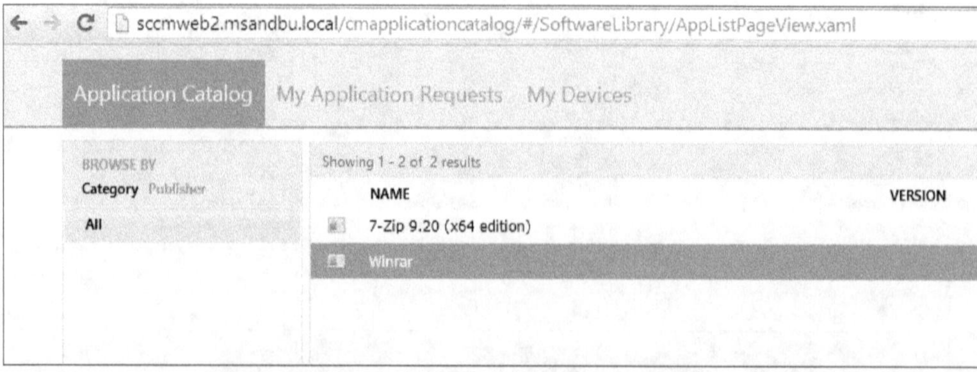

5. We can now see that the service is functional on the new URL. We can now change the default URL in the client policy to be the new load-balanced service I just created. As shown in the following screenshot, this can be altered under **Computer Policy** | **Computer Agent** | **Default Application Catalog Website point** | **Specify an URL**:

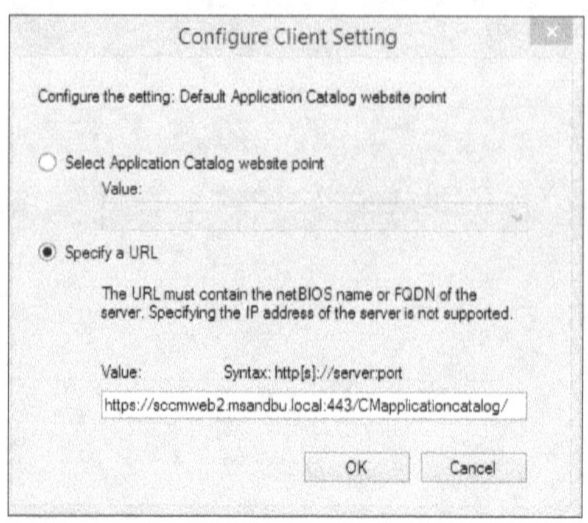

6. Then, we need to change the default client policy which we will deploy to the clients:

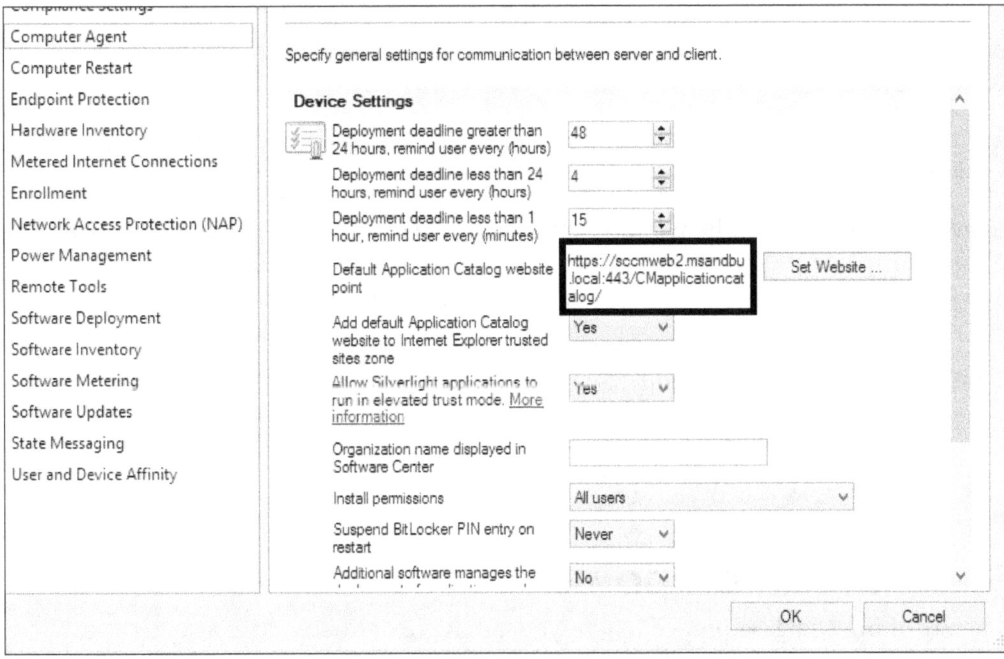

Application Catalog Web Service point

The Application Catalog Web Service point role is responsible to communicate between the site server database and the application catalog website. The web service point is referenced within the `web.config` file on the website point role, but one website point can only reference one web service point. In order to set up high availability for a web service point, you need to set up a load-balancing solution for the web service point, and then change the URL in `web.config` to point to the new URL. For instance, you can use Netscaler for this type of load balancing.

Define the URL under the client settings in the `web.config` file:

```
<client>
        <endpoint address="http://loadbalancedurl:80/CMApplicationCatalogSvc/ApplicationOfferService.svc"
        <endpoint address="http://loadbalancedurl:80/CMApplicationCatalogSvc/DeviceManagementService.svc"
</client>
```

Reporting Services point

The reporting point provides connectivity from the site server to a SQL Server Reporting Services to copy Configuration Manager reports to a specified report folder, to configure Reporting Services settings, and to configure Reporting Services security settings.

This role must be installed on a server with Microsoft SQL Server Reporting Services installed.

In order to ensure a highly available Reporting Service solution, you would need to set up multiple SQL Reporting Services and service points on top of that. This will give you multiple instances when generating reports within Configuration Manager.

> If you have multiple Reporting Services points and if you create a custom report against one instance, that report does not automatically synchronize with other reporting points, and in that case, we would have to copy the custom reports over to the other servers.

State Migration point

When running a task sequence where you can have defined a user's state capture task, the sequence will try to find a state migration point (within the boundary of the clients) where there is sufficient disk space. So, by having multiple state migration points within a site (or a boundary) we allow for multiple sources where a task sequence can place a user state.

System Health Validator point

Health Validator point is used to validate Configuration Manager's **Network Access Protection** (**NAP**) policies used for software updates. This role must be installed on a NAP health policy server.

To ensure high availability, you must set up multiple NAP servers with Health Validator points installed.

SMS Provider

The SMS Provider is a WMI provider that gives connectivity to the site database from the admin console. When you connect to a site using the Configuration Manager console, it will automatically choose an SMS Provider from the site. By installing multiple SMS providers within a site, you allow multiple access points for a client.

In order to install multiple SMS providers, you have to run Configuration Manager Setup application on the site server. This application can usually be found under the **Start** menu under the folder `Configuration Manager`. As shown in the following screenshot, choose **Perform Site maintenance or reset this site**:

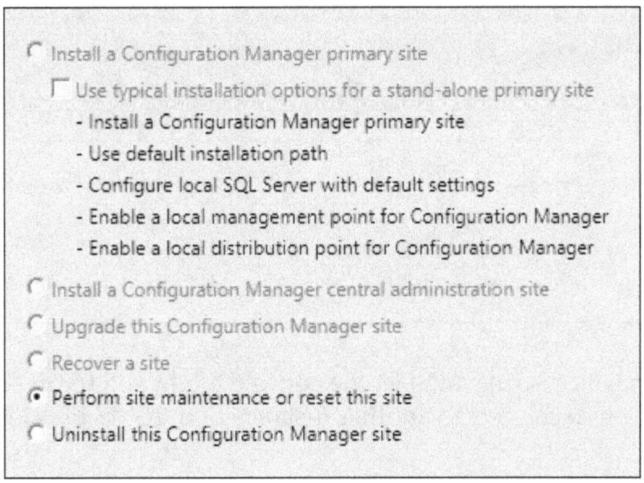

Now, choose **Modify SMS Provider Configuration**:

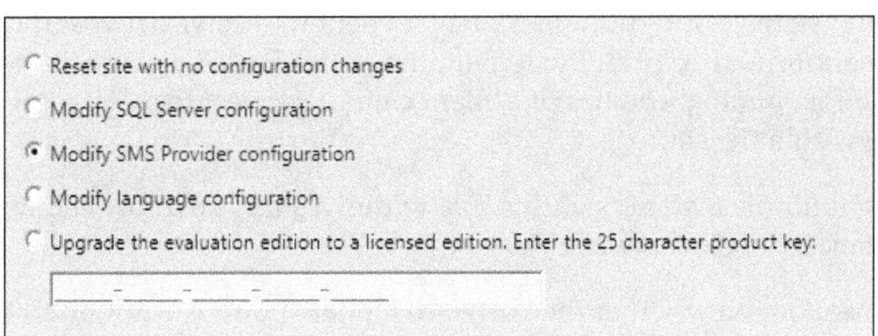

Then choose **Add a new SMS Provider**; here we need to enter a name of a blank in which we want to have the SMS Provider installed, as shown in the following screenshot:

> We need administration access on the remote server in order to install the role.

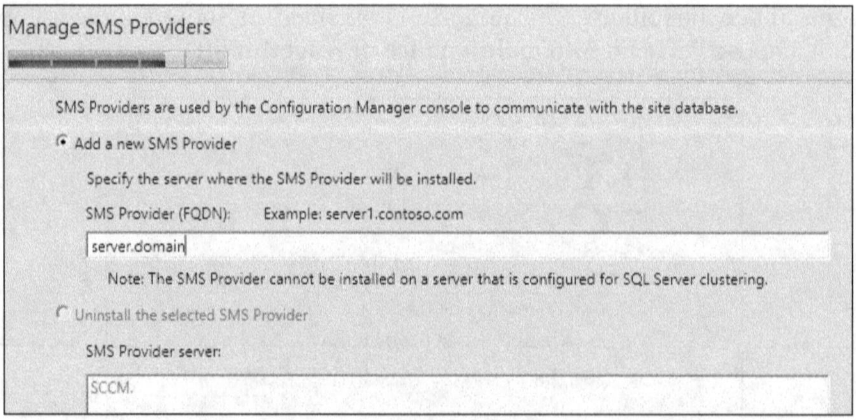

Note that if an instance is unavailable, the console might still try to connect to it. If you want to try to reconnect to another instance of the SMS Provider, just restart the console.

Software Update point

This point allows the Configuration Manager client to receive Microsoft updates from Microsoft through WSUS. By default, in Service Pack 1 a client chooses a random SUP for running updates; if a client cannot connect to a SUP, it will choose another one within the site.

By installing multiple instances of this role within a site, you allow clients to use another instance if one is unavailable.

It is also dependent on whether the Software Update point is configured to allow intranet-based clients, Internet-based clients, or both.

We can use the PowerShell cmdlet `Set-CMSoftwareUpdatePoint -NLBVIRTUALIP IPADRESS` to set up a load-balanced solution of the SUP.

If we want we can also deploy multiple Software Update points behind a single service using a load balancer, but in most cases a single Software Update point switching will suffice. If we have a pre Service Pack 1 environment, we could set up an NLB-based WSUS cluster that shares a SQL database located on a remote SQL Server or on the SQL Server where the site database resides. More information can be found in the following technet article:

`http://technet.microsoft.com/en-us/library/hh237369.aspx`

> WSUS 4.0 is included as default in Windows Server 2012 which uses other ports such as 2008 R2. The new default ports are 8530/HTTP and 8531/HTTPS, so make sure that the SUP talks to the right ports when you set this up. Also, WSUS in Windows Server 2012 does not support SQL Server 2012 Service Pack 1 at the time of this writing.

Client

This section is not about how to set up high availability for a Configuration Manager client, but how it operates and how it communicates with the site and some of the features is possesses.

It is important to note that clients do to not require continuous connection with any site server or server role.

Clients use any available instance in a site to perform an action; if a role is not available, the client will try to contact another instance of that role or until an instance is available.

Clients will locally cache its policies and actions (including software inventory, hardware inventory, software metering, and software advertisements) or any scheduled actions. So, if you have scheduled a hardware inventory every day and the management points are unavailable for the clients to report back data to, the data will be cached locally until a management point is available in the site again.

If a client cannot contact a management point or register with its site, it will contact the specified fallback status point and notify it.

Clients also have a built-in self-repair task which runs on a specified schedule. This is located in **Task Scheduler** under the `Configuration Manager` folder as shown in the following screenshot:

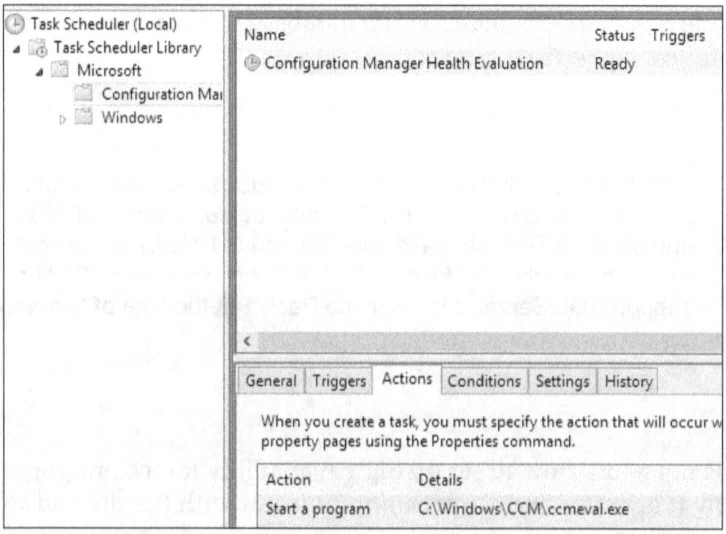

This task runs an executable called `ccmeval.exe` which is located in the client folder of Configuration Manager.

The task checks all the different components and all the prerequisites needed to have a functional client. You can view all the rules that the tasks use to evaluate that the health of the client is located in `ccmeval.xml`.

> It is not supported to modify the `ccmeval.xml` file.

You can also view the status of the client by checking the applet under Configuration Manager in Control Panel. From here, you can view which site and management point the clients are currently connected to. The information that the client shows here is gathered from registry under `HKLM\Software\Microsoft\SMS` and under `HKEY_LOCAL_MACHINE\Software\Microsoft\CCM`.

The client will also log in great detail all of the communication, policies that are run, or schedules these logs can be found in `C:\Windows\CCM\Logs`.

The files might look cryptic but they might contain valuable information when troubleshooting. Important logfiles to check when troubleshooting are given in the following table:

`AppDiscovery.log`	It detects installed application deployment types and if deployed deployment types are not installed
`AppEnforce.log`	It will show you the actual command line executed and the resulting exit code for each deployment type
`CAS.log`	It stands for **Content Access Service** and maintains the local cache on the client
`CcmEval.log`	It records client status evaluation activities
`CcmExec.log`	It records activities of the client and the SMS Agent Host service
`CcmMessaging.log`	It records activities which relate to communications between the client and management point
`CertificateMaintenance.log`	It maintains certificates for Active Directory domain services and management points
`CIDownloader.log`	It records details about configuration item definition downloads
`CITaskMgr.log`	It records tasks that are initiated for each application and deployment type, such as content download or install or uninstall actions
`ClientIDManagerStartup.log`	It creates and maintains the client GUID and identifies tasks performed during client registration and assignment
`ClientLocation.log`	It records tasks that are related to client-site assignment.
`ContentTransferManager.log`	It schedules the **Background Intelligent Transfer Service** (**BITS**) or the **Server Message Block** (**SMB**) to download or to access packages
`DataTransferService.log`	It records all BITS communication for policy or package access
`EndpointProtectionAgent.log`	It records information about the installation of the Endpoint Protection client and the application of antimalware policy to that client
`execmgr.log`	It records details about packages and task sequences that run on the client
`ExternalEventAgent.log`	It records the history of the endpoint protection agent
`FileBITS.log`	It records all package-access tasks
`InventoryAgent.log`	It records activities of software and hardware inventory on the agent

`LocationServices.log`	It records client activity for locating management points, distribution points, and software update points
`PolicyEvaluator.log`	It records details about the evaluation of policies on client computers
`SrcUpdateMgr.log`	It records activity for installed Windows Installer applications that are updated with current distribution point source locations

The logfiles should be viewed using `CMtrace.exe`, which can be found on the installation media of Configuration Manager under the folder `Tools`. This tool has built-in highlighting which makes it easier to find errors.

There are also some useful tools that can be used to troubleshoot a client. Microsoft has a set of tools which are a part of the System Center 2012 Configuration Manager Service Pack 1 Component Add-ons and Extensions pack, which can be download from `http://www.microsoft.com/en-us/download/details.aspx?id=36213`.

This pack includes a set of different tools such as:

- **Client Spy**: This can be used to troubleshoot software distribution and software metering
- **Policy Spy**: This can be used to view the set of client agent policies that are active on an agent
- **Power Viewer Tool**: This can be used to view the power management settings that are active on a client
- **Wakeup Spy**: This can be used to view *Wake-on-lan* functionality of a client

The package also includes other tools which are useful for migration purposes and for security purposes.

Sample site designs

As mentioned earlier in the chapter, we would be seeing some sample scenarios of how a site design might look like depending on how the business is set up for both geographical and business requirements.

It is always hard to make a sample design, this is all depending on what features the business needs and what requirements they have for availability.

These scenarios will always include the roles that are necessary and not the roles that are not required, but I will describe where I would place the different roles.

Scenario 1

We have a business called Alta IT which is an IT company based in a city in Norway called Alta.

The company has a single Active Directory domain and over 4,000 users, where most of the users have a desktop computer and a laptop. The service to the users will only be available on the internal network. They only have one location.

Some points that can be highlighted are as follows:

- Single location
- Single AD domain
- Intranet only
- Number of users

Design for this scenario might look like this:

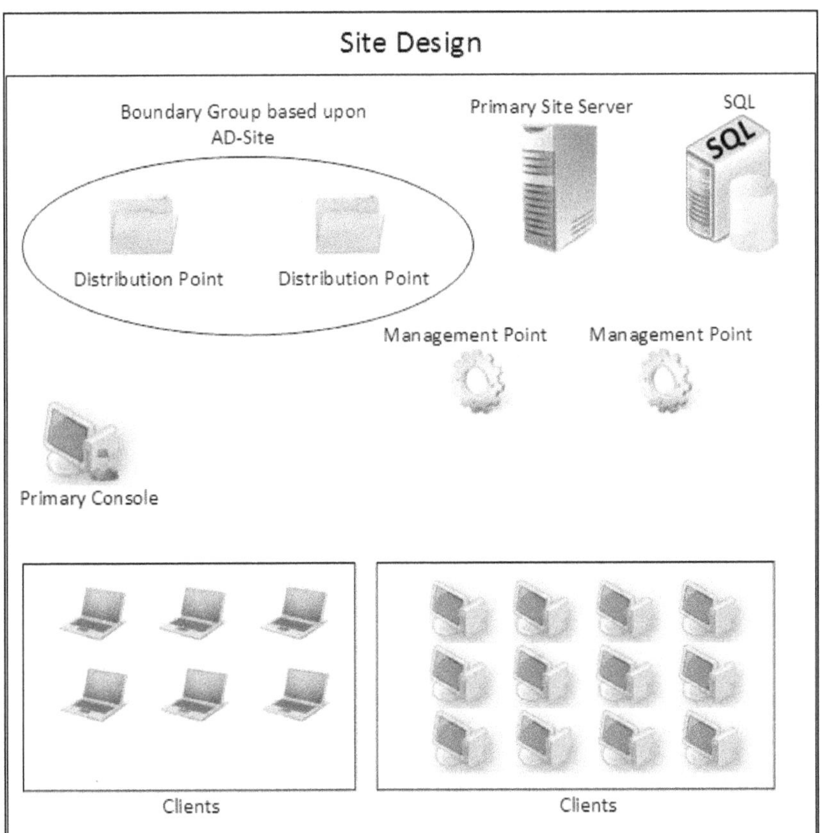

In this scenario, there is a single primary site, as the number of users is so small and with only one location, we only need a primary site. The number of clients exceeds the supported number of distribution points, and it is always recommend that we have two distribution points for a primary site solution. We could also place the distribution points within a boundary group where the boundary is set at the default Active Directory site where the clients are located.

The console will connect to the SMS Provider on the primary site server. The clients have two management points to which they can contact to download policies and reports in data. The primary site server is standalone and the SQL Server is standalone. If the business requires higher availability, we could set up a SQL cluster here as well to ensure availability of the site database.

Scenario 2

We have a business called Norway EDU which is an IT company, primary based in a city in Norway called Oslo. The company has three branch offices where most of the branch offices have above 200 users. The company has one domain with limited WAN bandwidth between the branch sites and the primary site. The primary site contains over 5,000 users. Each branch office is split up in its own Active Directory site. The primary site must sustain hardware failures in the database.

Some points that can be highlighted here are as follows:

- Multiple locations
- Limited bandwidth between locations
- Single domain with multiple sites
- Highly available SQL

The sample design might look like this:

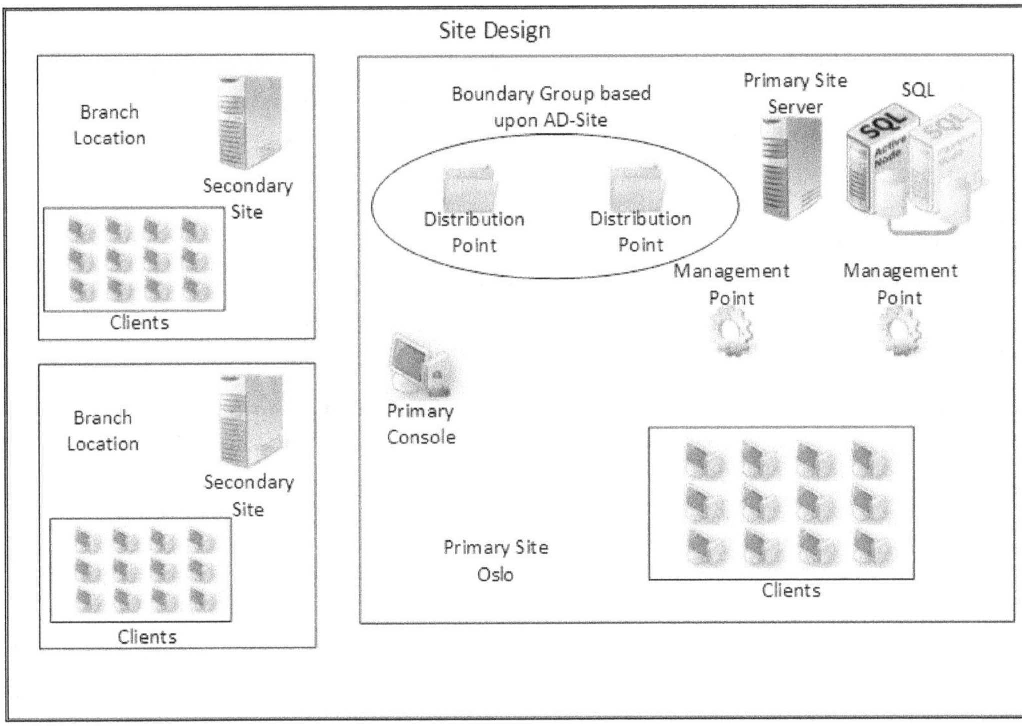

Since we have multiple branch offices which are connected via a low-bandwidth-based WAN, I used secondary sites in the branch offices. I did this because then I can make sure that clients do not try to use other management points in the site. If for instance, a client in the first branch office loses contact with its management point, it could potentially try to contact a management point in the second branch office. This would cause unnecessary traffic on both WAN links.

Secondary sites are not highly available, but can be restored from the primary site if needed.

With the secondary sites, a distribution point and one management point are also set up, and they are set up with boundary based on the Active Directory site for each location.

Also, we used a SQL cluster in the primary site and we can use RAID depending on what redundancy and performance we need on the cluster.

> Replication between a secondary site and a primary site uses the SQL Broker service port 4022 and this port needs to be opened in the firewall between the sites.

Scenario 3

Now based on the previous scenario, let's make some minor changes and see how they affect the design. What if instead of low-bandwidth links between the sites, we had fast LAN connections?

We could have exchanged the secondary sites with distribution points and set up one of the other distribution points in the primary site as a fallback distribution point for the branch office clients.

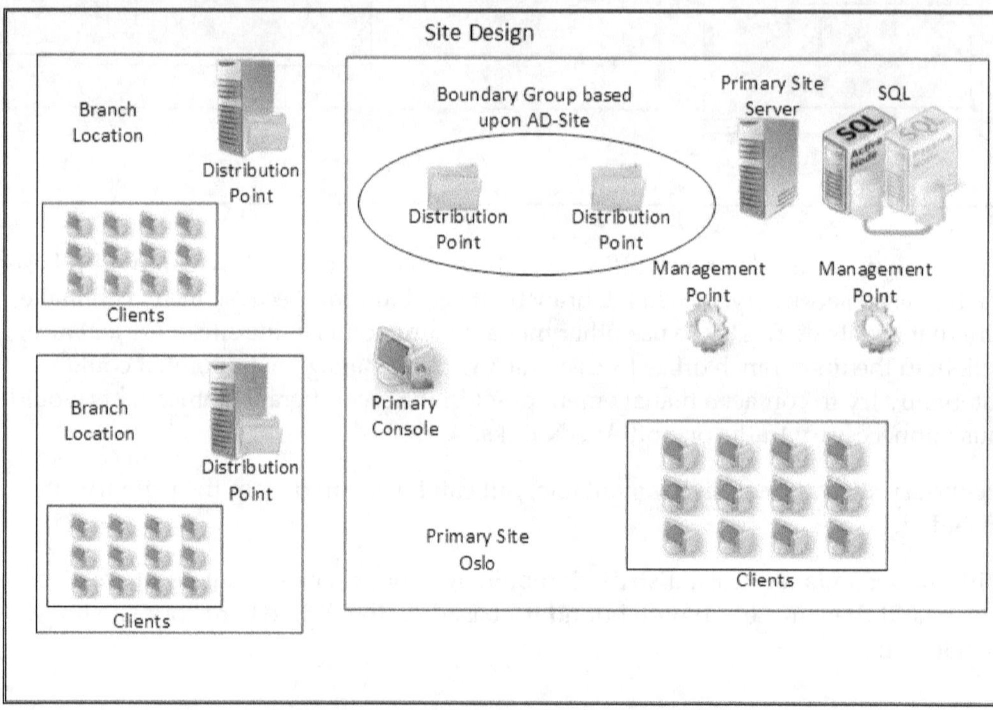

Here I would have set up boundary groups since there is an Active Directory site for each branch office, this would make sure that clients would connect to their distribution point within their location.

If we only had one Active Directory site, we could create a boundary-based distribution on the IP range of the branch offices.

Scenario 4

We have a business called Euro Corp, which is an IT company primarily based in London, UK.

The company has multiple sites around the globe with over 2,00,000 users globally.

The company has multiple Active Directory domains, where there is one domain in each of the sites and all the domains are within the same forest. There is a high-speed WAN link between all of the sites.

The main office has around 80,000 clients and the rest are spread around four different branch offices.

Some points that can be highlighted here are as follows:

- Multiple locations
- Number of users
- Multiple domains

A scenario like this looks a lot like what Microsoft IT themselves had to deploy for.

Since we have over 1,00,000 clients, we would need to have a CAS hierarchy, as a primary site only supports up to 1,00,000 clients. For the scenario here, we are assuming that each branch office has around 30,000 clients. Then, we have one site with 80,000 clients and four branch offices with 30,000 clients; this would leave us with five primary sites.

The following diagram shows what a sample design would look like for this scenario:

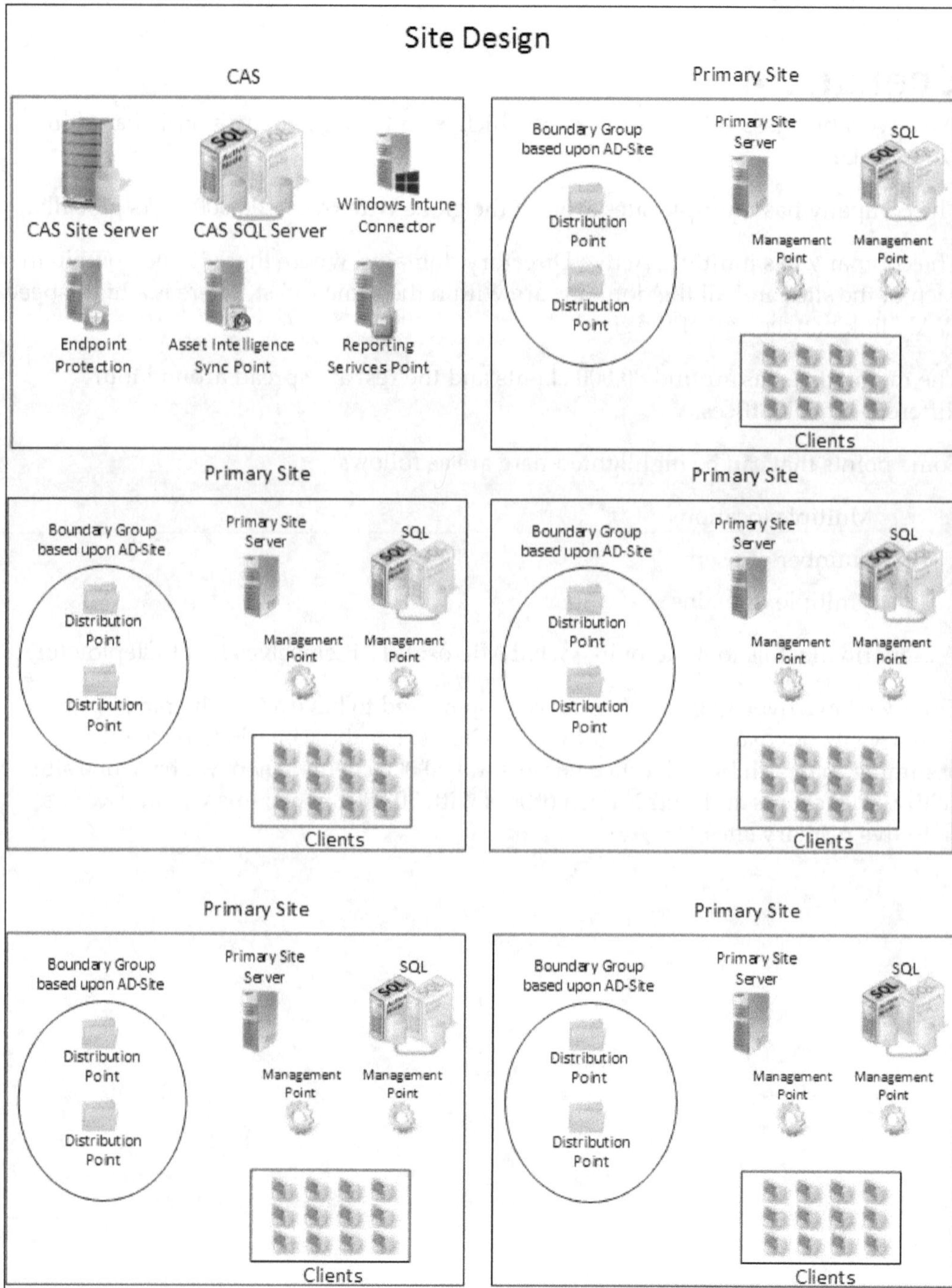

Some things worth taking note of. There are some of roles that can only be deployed in top of the hierarchy, these include:

- Windows Intune Connector
- Endpoint Protection
- Asset Intelligence Synchronization Point
- Reporting Services Point

(The reason why this is placed in the top role is that all the data from each primary site is synced to the CAS database and therefore we can generate reports from all the different sites from the CAS.) We can also install Reporting Services point on each primary site, but the data will only contain data from that particular primary site.

Now, the SQL cluster SAN drives should be set up as we described in *Chapter 1, Planning for High Availability with Configuration Manager*, where we split up different components of the SQL services on different drives with different RAID levels.

For each of the primary sites, we could also deploy a SQL cluster, all depending on what kind of availability and performance we wanted.

For one of the primary sites which has up to 80,000 users, we would have the following roles to support the load:

- 4x Management Points (supports 25,000 clients per management point)
- 20x Distribution Points (supports 4000 clients per distribution point)

The distribution points can be grouped into boundaries that are aware of Active Directory site, as each site has its own domain and then we can use the default site name for the clients as a boundary.

It is also important here to locate the CAS as close as possible to the primary site which has the most clients as it generates the maximum data in order to have the most-efficient bandwidth usage between the sites.

Scenario 5

Let's go back to scenario 1, where we had all the clients located in a single geographical location and network and on a single domain. If we changed some of the requirements for the company and moved some of the clients, the company sees that it needs more distribution points to the site to handle the load and also create a cloud-based solution to serve Internet-based clients, as they do not want to have distribution points facing to the Internet. Also, they want to move some of the load from the site servers to the distribution points themselves because they have moved some of the clients to another location.

So, for this scenario, we can use a cloud-based distribution point, and in order to allow clients to use a cloud service, we need to allow this in the client policy settings.

With the flexibility by using a cloud-based distribution points, we can deploy content to the cloud securely without exposing too much of our infrastructure to the Internet.

Also, we will set up a pull-based distribution point on the remote location in order to remove some of the load from the site server when deploying content to the site.

It is important to note that when we set up a distribution point as pull-based, it will ignore the rate limiting options that are set.

Also, we placed a management point in the DMZ zone which allows Internet-based clients to communicate with the site.

Some components that I did not include in the design is the PKI infrastructure which needs to deploy secure communication between the clients and the site, and from the clients to the cloud-based distribution point.

The deployment of these roles will mostly be covered in the next chapter.

The following is the sample design:

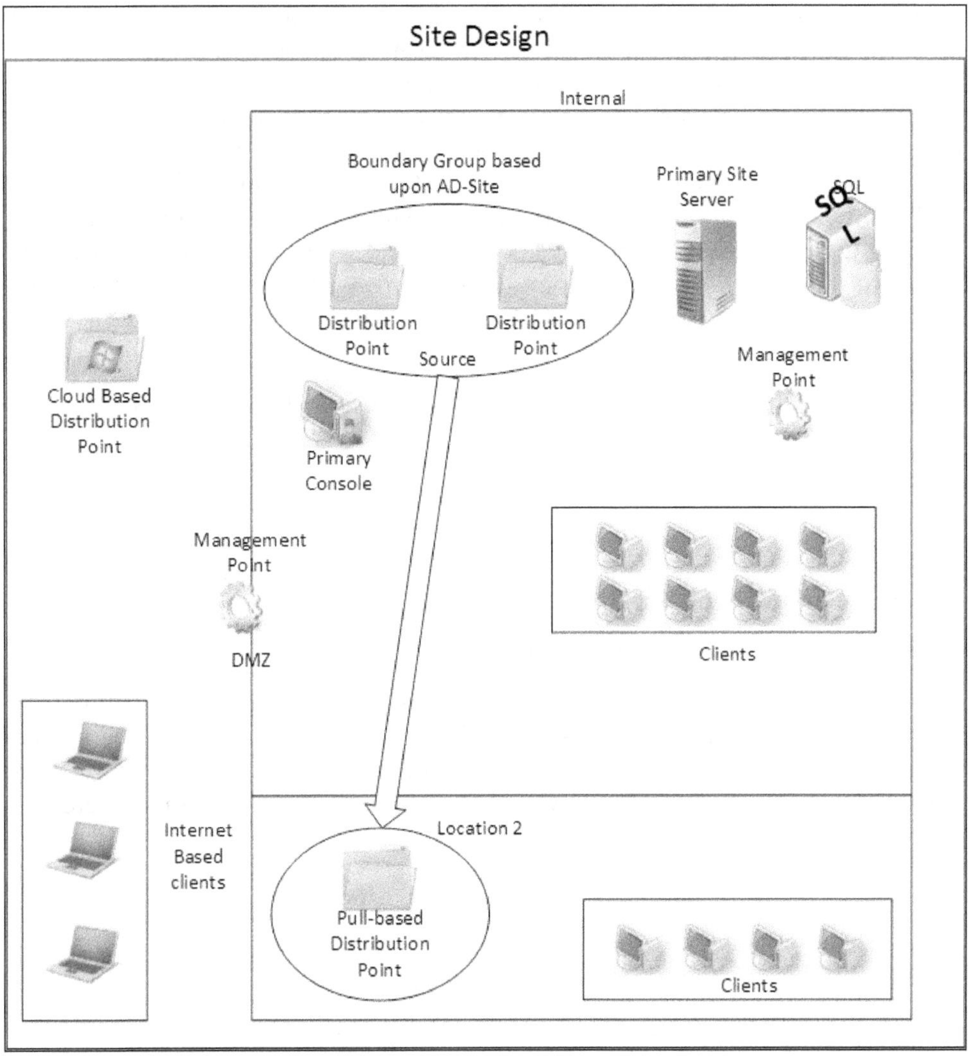

Scenario 6

We have a company called TGI IT which is located in Norway, with multiple remote sites. The company has around 800 users—it has around 500 users in the primary site, around 100 users in the largest branch offices, and 20 in the smaller branch sites. The company has a strict company policy around security and wants a design to reflect that. The company has one Active Directory domain and one site for the largest branch office, and every computer is part of the domain. Different sites have a good bandwidth available in the primary site. This company is currently looking to expanding their businesses to involve the cloud, and want the users to have access to the service while roaming. The company needs to restrict the amount of data being moved during business hours because the branch office users access services from the primary site.

There are some important points to take note of here, which are as follows:

- Multiple locations
- High level of security
- Cloud adaption
- Small number of users
- Reduced amount of bandwidth usage during business hours

There are a lot of factors to include for this site design. First, we need to think how can we secure this service in the most feasible manner. Since clients will be available to be managed from the Internet, we need to set up a design which reduces the need to expose roles to the Internet. Also, we have multiple remote locations where we need to reduce the amount of bandwidth used.

As shown in the following diagram, depending on the link between **Branch Location 1** and **Primary Site Server**, you might need to place a distribution point at the site:

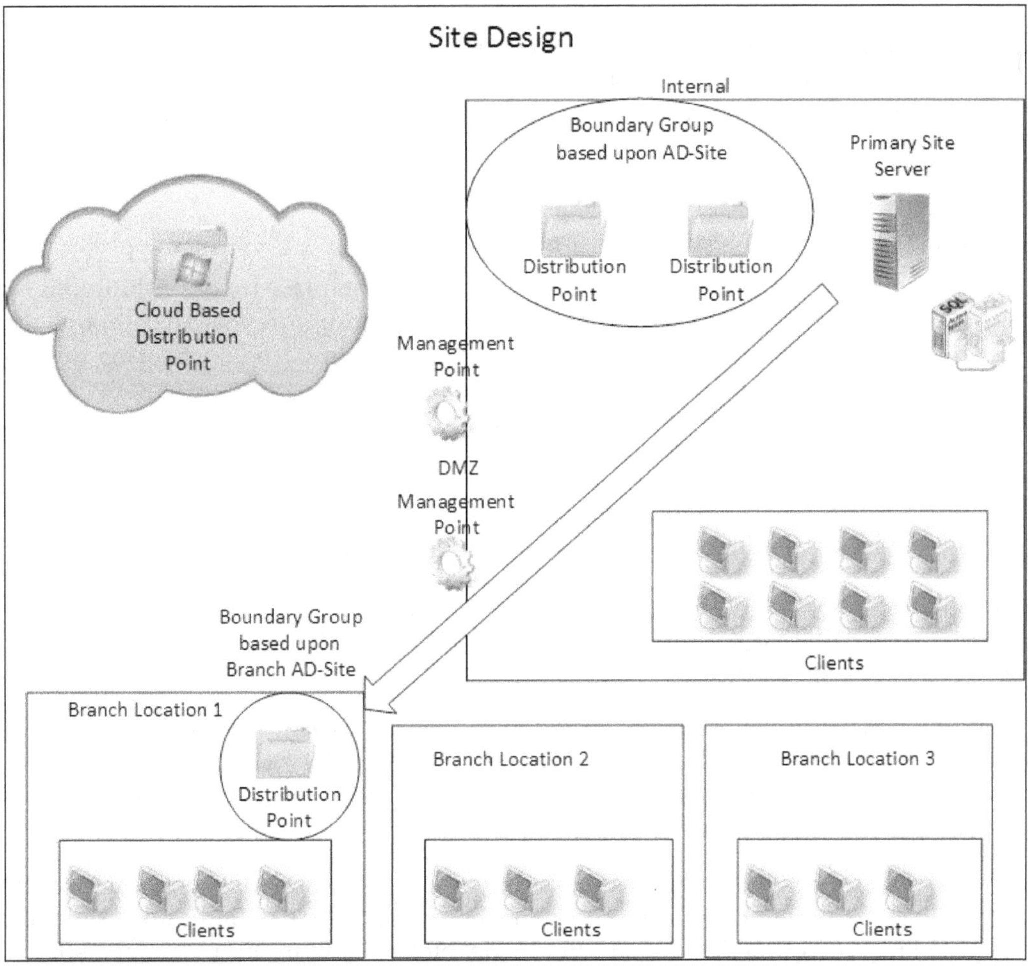

Here, we also need to activate rate limiting on the branch distribution point in order to limit the bandwidth usage during business hours. We can define that Internet-based clients are allowed to use cloud-based distribution points, and that internal distribution points are only allowed to access internally.

Since the branch locations have sufficient bandwidth to communicate back to the primary site, we do not need to establish more distribution points.

If the business sees that the branch offices are overusing the WAN link between offices, consider creating a boundary based upon the IP range of the branch offices, and deploy a distribution point at each branch office.

Another option here would be to use Direct Access for the remote clients, this way we would have an IPsec tunnel between the infrastructure and the remote clients, and then clients could securely connect with the distribution points without exposing them remotely.

Monitoring

A crucial component (even if we have high availability in place for our solution) is the ability to have a good overview of the solution. Making sure that all components are working as they should without having to go into monitoring or checking the event, log in to all site servers. Microsoft also implemented some new features in Service Pack 1, which allows us to create notifications for all alerts which occur within Configuration Manager.

But most times, we have another monitoring solution in place, such as Operations Manager, which is another product within the System Center portfolio.

Operations Manager allows us to get an overview of the entire infrastructure, going from hardware, network, storage, to different operating systems and applications, and services running on top.

Microsoft has made custom packs (called management packs) which allows us to monitor different Windows components such as, AD, DNS, DHCP, Fileserver, and Exchange. They have also created different packs for System Center components including Configuration Manager.

By using Operations Manager for monitoring of Configuration Manager you can get a good insight into your solution. The management pack for Configuration Manager is created by the product team that actually develops Configuration Manager, so you will get a monitoring solution with best upon best practice from Microsoft.

If you have Operations Manager in place in your infrastructure, you can download the Configuration Manager Management Pack from `http://www.microsoft.com/en-us/download/details.aspx?id=34709`.

Summary

Now, we have gone through different roles and features within Configuration Manager and how we can deploy them as highly available. Also, we have seen which roles cannot be deployed as highly available.

Also, we have seen in this chapter how clients locate their site and management points from different sources within the infrastructure and how clients locate their content based on where the client resides.

We also went through some sample site designs for how a deployment might look like for different scenarios, and how we can place and scale roles within the design.

It is important to know what the scalability of a role is, as this gives you a good pinpoint on how many of each roles you need for the number of clients to handle the load.

Remember that a design should always be designed based upon business requirements and what features are needed.

In the next chapter, we will take a closer look at the backend roles that are needed for Configuration Manager and how we set them up redundantly.

3

Deploy Highly Available Backend Services

So far we have gone through different components within Configuration Manager, what features they have, which features they support, and how we can deploy them as highly available. Even if we have a highly available Configuration Manager solution, we still need to think of the other services on which it is dependent such as AD, SQL, DNS, and DHCP. Of course some services are more important than others, but it is important to realize what options we have to implement other features as highly available within our infrastructure.

In this chapter, we will be covering the following topics:

- We will go through how Configuration Manager uses Active Directory and how we can set up a redundant Active Directory and DNS solution
- We will set up a redundant DHCP service
- We will set up a failover cluster running Microsoft SQL Server and see what other options we have
- What options we have for setting up a redundant PKI solution using AD CS

Active Directory

Configuration Manager relies heavily on Active Directory for many of its functions. Active Directory is responsible for handling every authentication process which takes place within a Windows environment. Every user and computer has its own associated object and a password attached to it within the domain.

Each time a user wants to log in to a domain and presses *Ctrl + Alt + Delete*, the clients send over 10 different requests to the domain. So, if we have a high number of clients and users within the domain, we will have a lot of traffic going to the domain services.

Configuration Manager uses Active Directory for a lot of features, such as authentication to the service itself, application deployment, role-based access control, remote tools, and reporting.

Domain Controllers is the server role that handles Active Directory, every authentication process, user changes, password updates, and queries are handled by the domain controllers. So, when setting up a redundant Active Directory solution, we need to have multiple domain controllers available for the clients and other services that are dependent on it.

When a client computer wants to establish a connection with Active Directory, it looks in its DNS server to find a LDAP SRV record within the zone for the domain, the client with send a query to DNS for this record `_ldap._tcp.domainname`, and if there are multiple domain controllers listed with that record, the client will look for the one with the lowest weight value. If there are multiple records with the same weight, it will choose a random one. If the client is placed within a custom Active Directory site, the first domain controller will look at the IP address the client is located on and return a request to the client stating which domain controller it should contact.

After a client has established a connection with a domain controller and domain joining process is complete, the client will cache the domain controller's information for future usage. If that particular domain controller goes down, the client will again go to the DNS zone and look for available domain controllers.

When we have multiple domain controllers within our environment, they will automatically set up and start replicating and synchronizing data between them. Domain controllers have built-in mechanisms to ensure that every object (for instance, users, group, and machine accounts) is in sync, and that requests are load balanced between domain controllers.

Domain controllers are set up with different roles. One of them and the most important role is the global catalog. The global catalog is a service that is needed to log in a multiple-domain forest, as it holds information regarding universal groups from other domains. Even though you do not need a global catalog server to log in locally to the domain it resides in, it is still advisable to have one.

> When setting a new Active Directory, the first domain controller is always set up as a global catalog.

There are other roles as well which a domain controller might have. These roles are known as the **FSMO** (**Flexible Single Master Operation**) roles. These roles are:

- Schema Master
- Domain Naming Master
- **Primary Domain Controller** (**PDC**) Emulator
- RID Master
- Infrastructure

The Schema Master role is the one responsible for performing updates to the directory schema. This server is the only one that can perform updates to the directory schema. Once you have done a schema extension to this server, it will replicate to other domain controllers in the domain (therefore you need to perform Configuration Manager schema extension on this server). You can only have one of these roles in an Active Directory forest. In order to see which server has this role, you need to add the schema snap-in by running the command `regsvr32 schmmgmt.dll`. This will add a new snap-in called Active Directory Schema.

The **Domain Naming Master** role is the one responsible for updating domain names or adding domain names within a forest. So, in order to add or remove a domain from a forest, the server holding this role must be available. You need only one domain naming master for a forest.

The **PDC Emulator** role is the one responsible for performing password updates and it is a default controller for performing group policy updates and maintaining account lockouts. Also, if a logon authentication fails at another domain controller due to a bad password, the server will forward the authentication request to the PDC to validate the request against data it has. This role is also responsible for syncing the clocks with other domain controllers in the domain. This server needs to be accessible at all times and is the server with the most load of the FSMO servers.

The **RID Master** role is responsible for allocating a unique ID for every object within Active Directory. Each time we create a user or object within Active Directory, it is allocated a unique **RID** (**Relative ID**) which is handed to the domain controller from the RID master. We can only have one RID master for each domain and if this server goes down, we cannot create new objects within Active Directory.

The **Infrastructure** role is responsible for updating references from objects in its domain to objects in other domains. The role is the FSMO role which is responsible for updating an object's SID and unique name in a cross-domain reference. There can only be one infrastructure role in each domain.

All of these roles make up an Active Directory service. When we install a new domain controller in a new forest, all these roles will be placed on the same domain controller.

We can install a new domain controller by using Server Manager (if we already have a domain controller installed previously). Navigate to **Manage** | **Role Based or Feature Based** | **Active Directory Domain Services** | **Install**.

> This will only install the role and not configure it. We have to run the configuration wizard from server manager to configure it correctly. We can also install the Active Directory role using PowerShell by using the following cmdlet:
>
> ```
> Install-WindowsFeature -name AD-Domain-Services
> -IncludeManagementTools
> ```

When we start the configuration wizard, we have to choose **Add to an existing domain**. By default it will also add the DNS role and configure it as a global catalog.

We can also add it to a site if we wish (sites are useful if your infrastructure or business is large spanning over different networks or that you have branch offices), as you can see in the following screenshot:

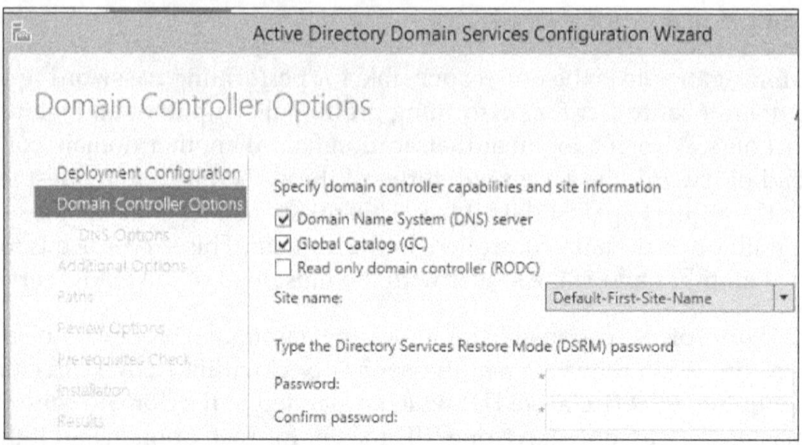

We can see which domain controller has the different FSMO roles by running the command `netdom query fsmo` from command prompt.

But these roles have some limitations, because you cannot set up these roles as highly available or with any form for redundancy. In case of a critical failure in one of these roles and if we need to transfer the role from old server to a new domain controller, this procedure is called **seizing**. This should only be done if we cannot restore the original domain controller, and the old server that had the role should not be connected to the network again.

In order to do this, we need to use the command-line utility for Active Directory called `NTDSUTIL`.

We can start this either from the domain controller or if we have **RSAT** (**Remote Server Administration Tools**) installed on another computer.

So, to ensure a highly available Active Directory, make sure that we have multiple domain controllers within the domain to service different clients and services. Also, make sure that you have multiple global catalog servers as well as some services and queries that require a global catalog server.

DNS

Another component that Active Directory and Configuration Manager and other roles are very dependent on is DNS.

DNS is responsible for translating IP addresses to hostnames and is essential in every infrastructure.

When installing Active Directory, you also get the option to install DNS as part of the installation because you need DNS in place to set up Active Directory. By installing DNS as a part of Active Directory, you have the ability to use the replication features of Active Directory to replicate DNS records from one domain controller to another (this is known as **Active Directory-Integrated Zones**). You also gain some features with this setup when clients try to update their own DNS information (this is known as **Secure Dynamic Updates**).

DNS is a basic network service that operates on UDP port 53, which makes it easy to set it up as a load-balanced service. We can use Netscaler as well to set up a load-balanced DNS service.

First, we need to add the servers which have the DNS role installed under server's panel, as shown in the following screenshot:

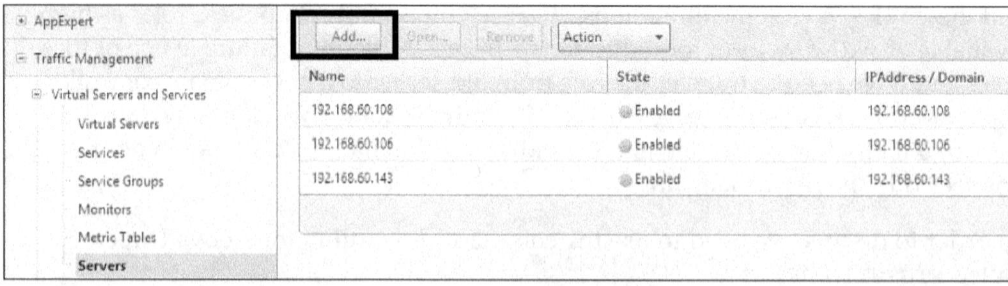

Next, we need to add the DNS service under **Services** and choose a monitor which checks if the DNS server is responding or not. (If a server does not respond to the monitor, it will be marked as offline for the load-balanced service). We need to create a service for each server we wish to load balance. This is because under **Services** we bind a specific service to a server, as you can see in the following screenshot:

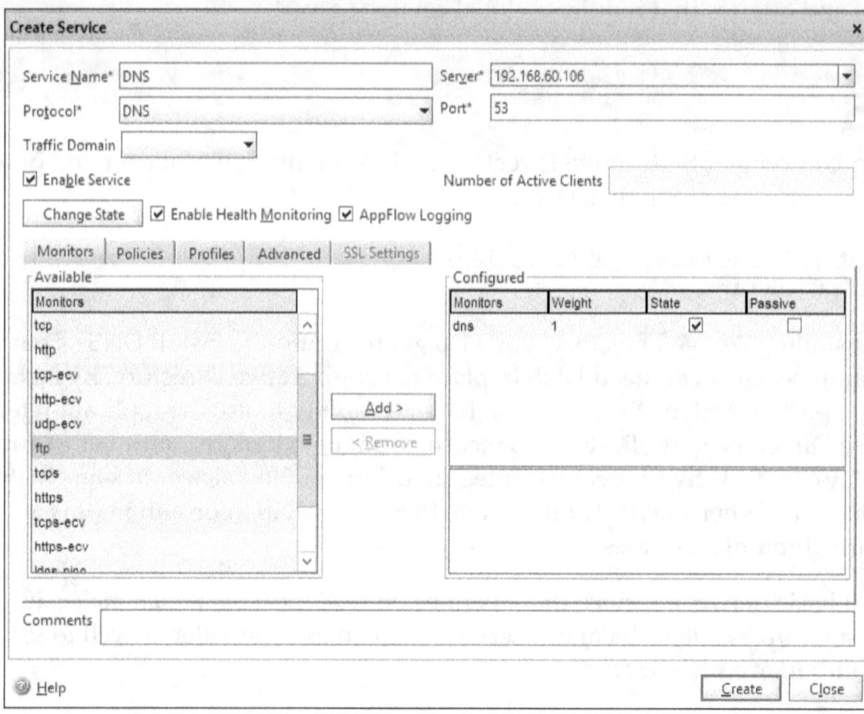

Next, we need to create a new virtual service where we will attach all the different DNS servers to a new IP address, and to even the load of the servers in the backend, we will choose a session based on least-connections connections:

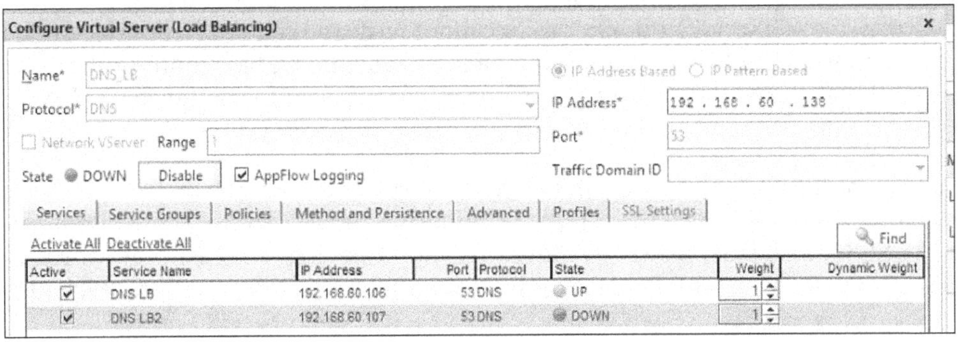

Now that we have a new load-balanced DNS service on the IP **192.168.60.138**, we can use this IP address when we need to set up new servers/clients with network IP configuration.

If we have not set up a load-balanced DNS service, we can set up a preferred DNS server and an alternate DNS server on each host. The downside with this is that if multiple DNS servers are down, it might take time for the client to contact a DNS server that is functional. It is also best practice to configure the client to default register the connection addresses in DNS under the **DNS** pane, as this allows for easier management and removal of stale records.

It is important to note that when configuring these settings for a DNS server, we should add its own loopback address as an alternate DNS server, as you can see in the following screenshot:

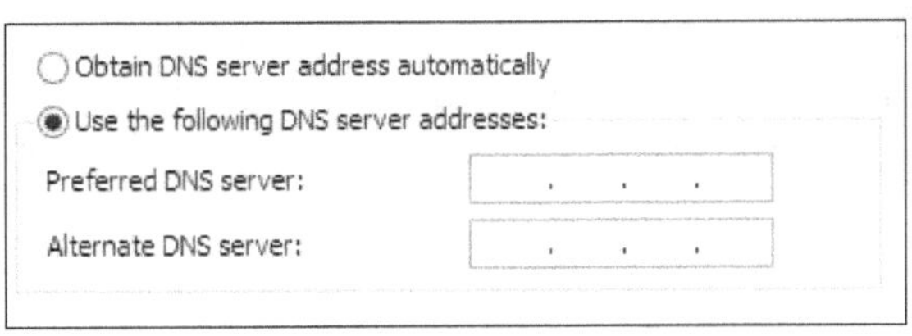

SQL Server

Another important role to configure redundant is SQL Server.

The SQL Server role is responsible for the site server database, so if the SQL Server goes down, the site server and other roles cannot write or read data from the database. Microsoft SQL Server has different forms of high availability, but Configuration Manager only supports Microsoft SQL Cluster. But we need to configure this before we start installing Configuration Manager.

There are multiple ways we can set up this cluster but I have chosen to set it up using SMB 3-based storage. Since the release of Windows Server 2012, it is now supported to place SQL databases on SMB 3 shares. Instead of having shared storage directly attached to the SQL servers, we set up file server which has the storage attached and set up the file server with SMB shares which the SQL Servers will access.

By leveraging the SMB protocol, we do not need to connect every server via an **Internet Small Computer System Interface (iSCSI)** network or FC network to the SAN, but we can use the existing network for the traffic.

We also have other features within SMB which makes it equally as good as iSCSI both in bandwidth capabilities and high-availability features. The following is an example design for an SMB-based solution:

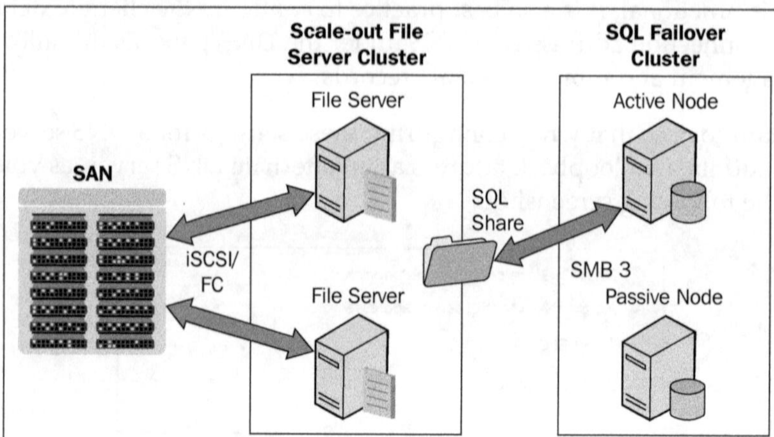

When settings up this type of solution, we need to have a clustered file server solution in place before we start with the SQL cluster. In order to implement a clustered SQL server, there are a couple of things we need to do before we can properly configure it.

> I will not be covering how to implement a highly-available file server. We will only cover how we can set up an SQL cluster against an SMB-file-based solution.

Windows SQL Server standard supports a two-node-based SQL cluster which will be the most likely scenario for most cases (remember that SQL Standard only supports up to 50,000 clients). Before we can start configuring SQL, we need to install the failover cluster role on each node. This can be done via Server Manager.

> We can run the command `Install-WindowsFeature -Name Failover-Clustering -IncludeManagementTools` from PowerShell to install this feature as well.

After the feature is installed, we have to create a cluster before we can add roles to it. Start **Failover Cluster Manager** and right-click and choose **Create Cluster...** as shown in the following screenshot:

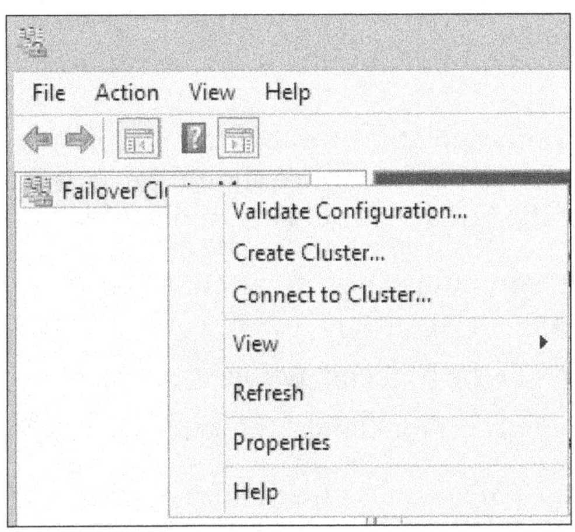

Next, we need to choose which servers are going to participate in the cluster. Each server on the list needs to have failover clustering installed, as you can see in the following screenshot:

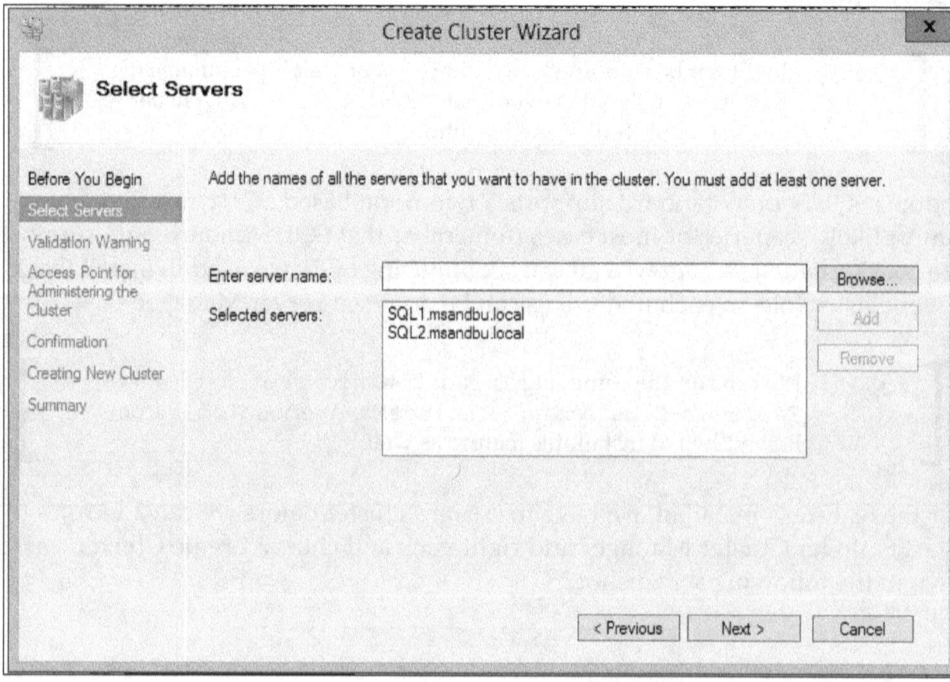

Remember that the servers need at least two different NICs in order to set up properly. For a production deployment, we should have defined the following three NICs where all of the NICs of the cluster nodes are accessible to each other:

- 1x for Heartbeat communication between the cluster nodes (this can be a private network)
- 1x for connection to the backend storage
- 1x for public connection for clients and resources which need to access it

Before a cluster is created, we need to run a validation report against it. Microsoft will only support a cluster if it is validated first. Choose **Yes** and then choose only the tests I have selected in the following screenshot and skip the tests for **Storage**.

(Because the data will be stored on a SMB share and the servers only have locally attached storage to it, the cluster validation will fail if we do not deselect **Storage**.) Mark the rest of the tests as shown in the following screenshot:

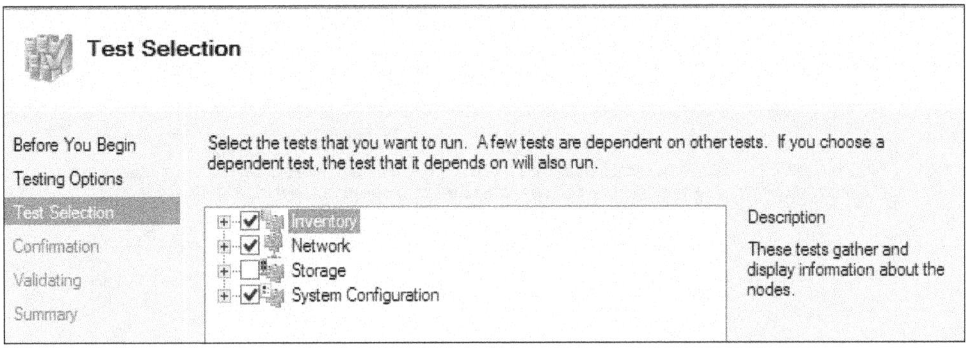

If we have set up everything correctly the cluster validation will return successfully, as you can see in the following screenshot:

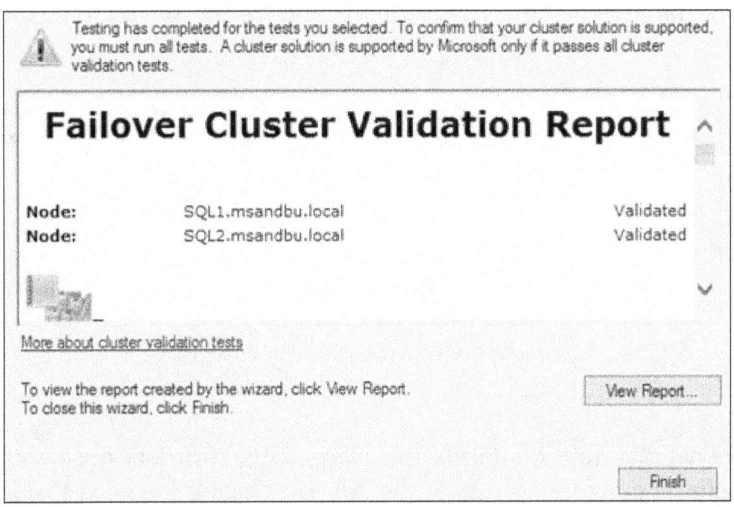

Next, we need to create an access point for the cluster. An access point is a name and an associated IP address. This address is used to administer the cluster and will not be the access point for the clients who wish to communicate with the SQL service. In the following screenshot we enter an access point:

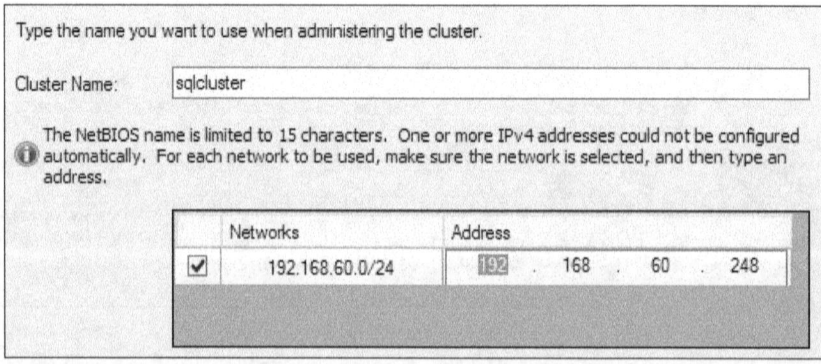

After this is done, we can continue on with the creation of the cluster. When this is complete, we have running Window Server failover cluster with no attached roles to it:

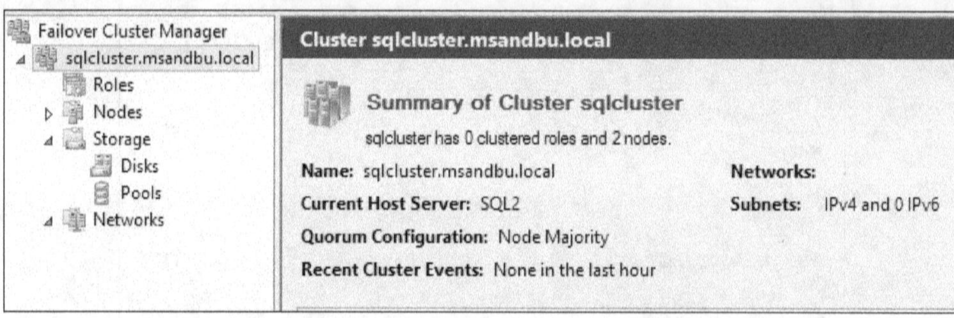

First thing we need to do is configure the usage of the different networks. If we have three defined networks set up in the failover cluster, we need to change the properties of these:

- 1x Heartbeat NIC should be changed to **Allow cluster network communication on this network**. This allows for the cluster nodes to speak to each other on this network.
- Change 1x Connection to the backend storage to **Do not allow cluster network communication on this network**.
- Change 1x Public **Connection for clients and resources** to **Allow clients to connect through this network**.

After we have configured the networks, we have to configure the quorum settings. The quorum for a cluster is the number of objects that needs to be online for that cluster to continue running.

By default, our cluster is now set up with the quorum **Node Majority**, so when one of our SQL Servers goes offline, the cluster goes offline. If we had three servers online and one went offline, the cluster would continue to run, as the number of running nodes is higher than the number of failed hosts. As we have two nodes in our cluster, we need to change quorum settings. Right-click on the cluster object, and go to **More Actions | Configure Cluster Quorum Settings**.

Here we need to add a witness to the cluster as shown in the following screenshot:

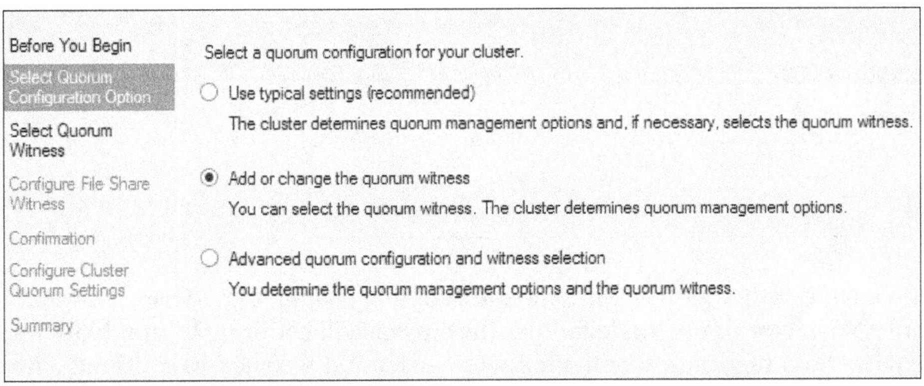

Since the only shared resource these two nodes have in common is the file share on our file server, we need to add a file-share-based witness:

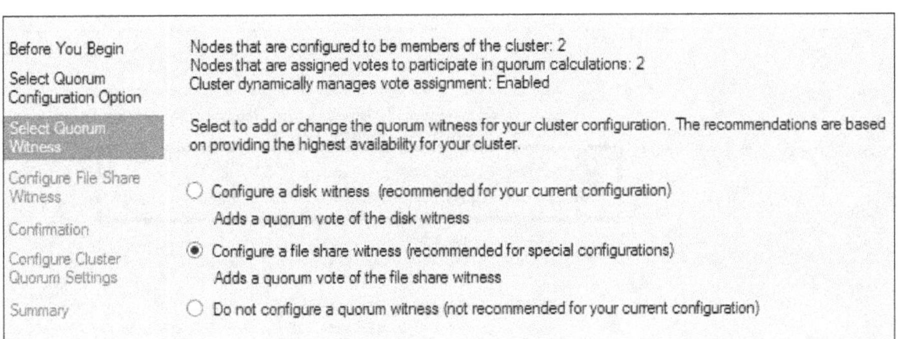

This will then add the file share to the quorum. Next, we need to specify the file share resource path.

It is important to note that the share we specify here is not used for any other data. The path cannot be a part of a DFS namespace and make sure that the cluster resource account has full access of the network path. Also, administrator needs full access on the share and NTFS rights on the folder.

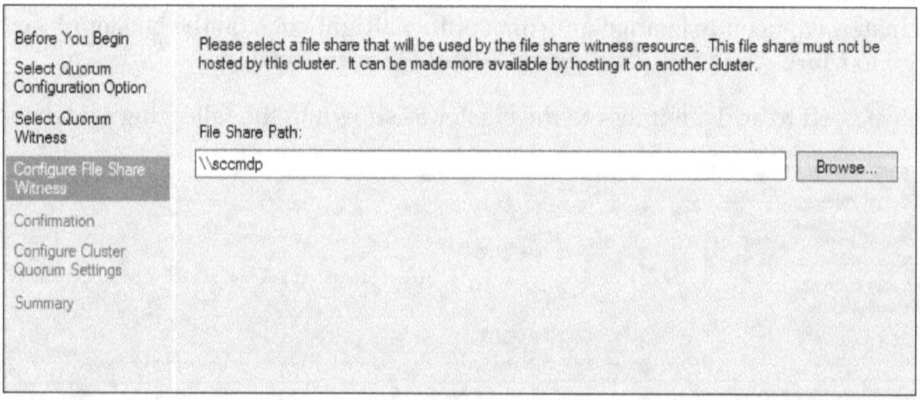

After we have added the file path, the quorom will change to node and file share majority, so in case of one node failure, the cluster will continue to run. Now we are done with the configuration of the failover cluster and we need to continue with the SQL installation.

From the SQL Media setup we can start installation of a SQL cluster, as shown in the following screenshot:

> Before we start the installation of the SQL Server, we should run the failover cluster validation wizard or we will get some warning messages during the setup. This is not crucial but should be done in order to validate that the cluster setup is done correctly.

This can be done from within **Failover Cluster Manager**, right-click on the cluster resource and click on **Validate Cluster**. When we start the installation of SQL, it will check if the cluster will validate and other prerequisites which are needed in order to set up a SQL cluster:

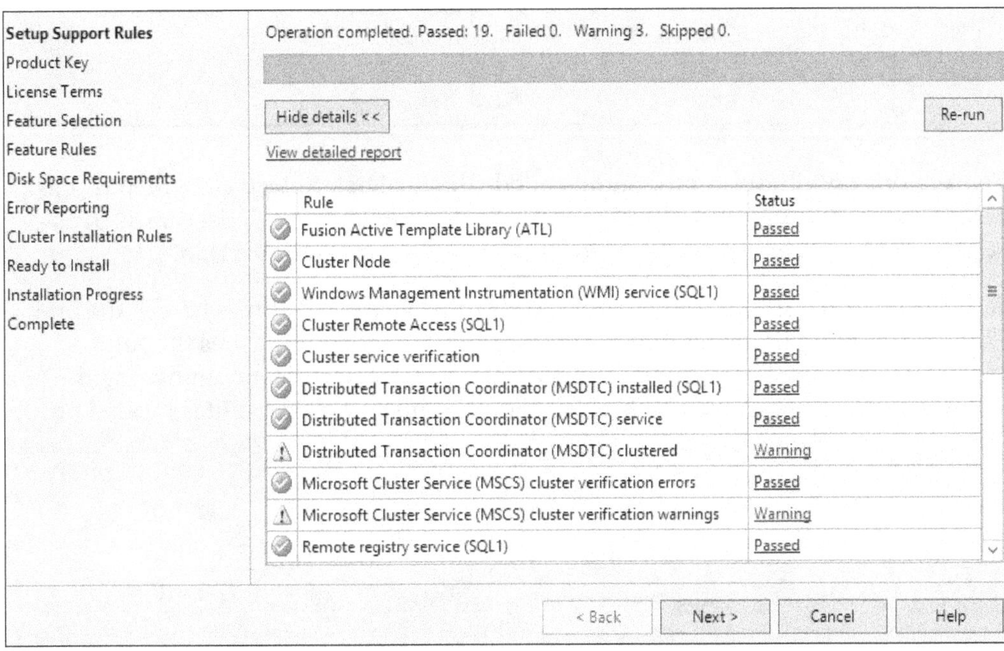

Next, we need to accept the license terms and enter a product key. Then we define which roles we are going to install on the cluster resource (Database Engine and Management Studio), and then we come to the cluster specific options.

First, we need to enter the instance name and the cluster resource name and where we should install the instance:

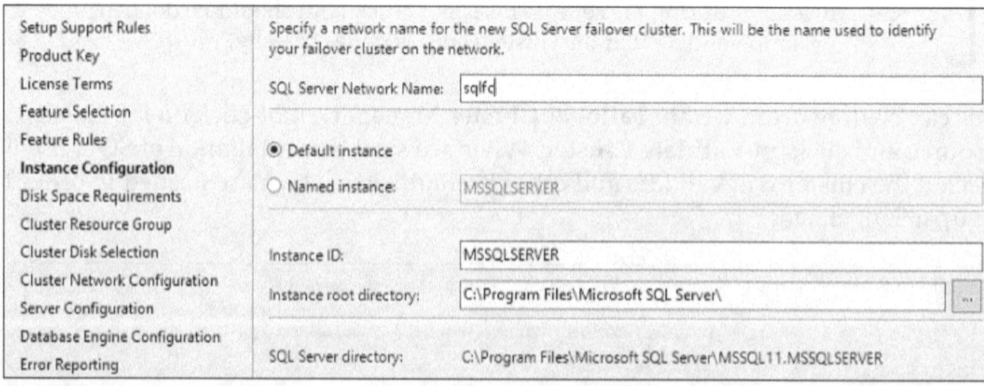

We have one option during the setup called **Cluster Disk Selection**, which is only viable if we had a shared connection solution directly to the SQL Servers such as iSCSI or FC. So, we can go directly to **Cluster Network Configuration**.

Here, we enter the information about the cluster role (the IP adress here is the one that Configuration Manager will communicate with when it finishes the setup correctly). As shown in the following screenshot, the network chosen here will be the same network as the one that the failover cluster access point is located on:

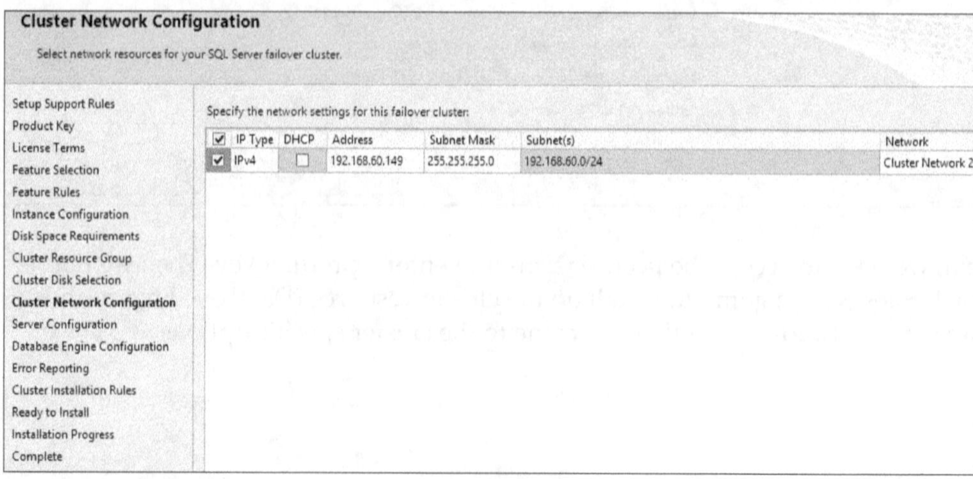

After that is done, we have to service account information. Note that the users here should be managed service accounts or restricted active directory users. We also need to define the right collation here. As you can see in the following screenshot, Configuration Manager only supports `SQL_Latin1_General_CP1_CI_AS`:

> The services are set up to start manually, this is because the services are going to be managed by the cluster resource itself.

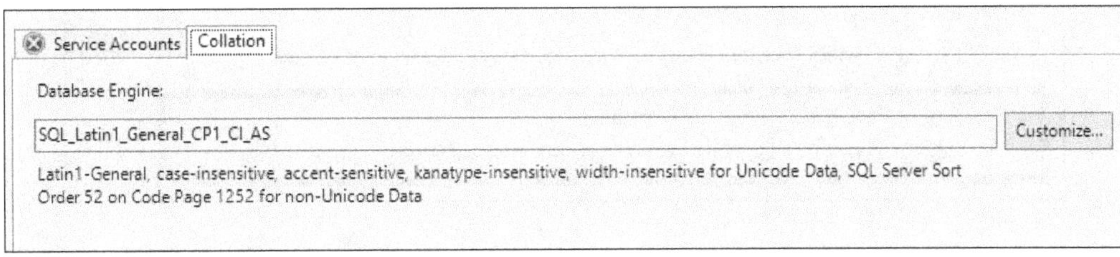

When we come to **Server Configuration**, we have to change the authentication mode to **Windows authentication** and make sure to add **Administrator** as a super user on the database solution.

Next, we go over to **Data Directories** and from here we need to change the location to **SMB share**.

This will place all system databases and newly created databases and logfiles on that share.

It is important to note that it is best practice to spread different components of a SQL database across different volumes. For instance, having `tempdb`, user database, and logfiles on different volumes to spread the load across different disks. This can be seen in more detail in *Chapter 1, Planning for High Availability with Configuration Manager*. The following screenshot shows the options in **Data Directories**:

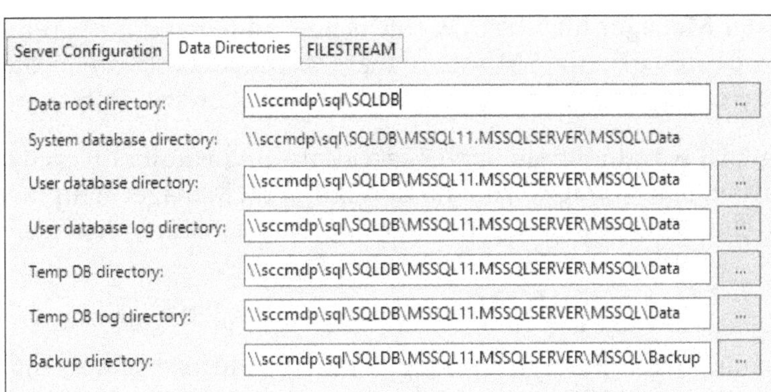

After that is done, we can finish the installation on the first node; when we want to start the installation of the second node, we need to choose **Add node to a SQL Server failover cluster**, as shown in the following screenshot:

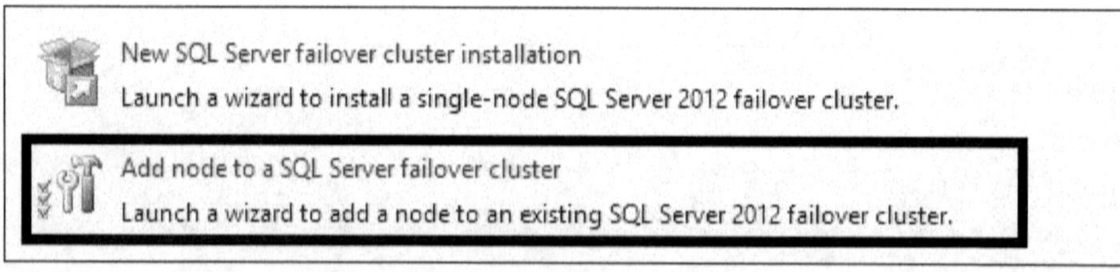

When you start the installation, it will automatically pick up the running cluster resource instance and it will show what instance is going to be set up as highly available and on which node this is running on now:

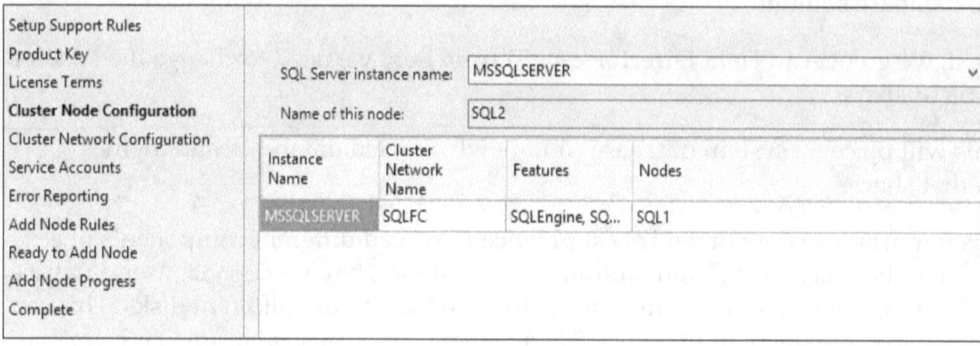

After this is done and the installation is complete, we can now see from within **Failover Cluster Manager** that the SQL role is now added and is operating on two nodes. Also, we can see on the SMB share that the system bases are located there, and when we create new databases, they will be placed on the SMB share.

It is important that we add the site server as a local administrator on each of the nodes in the SQL cluster. And when we run the Configuration Manager setup, we need to enter the SQL cluster name and not the failover cluster access point name.

DHCP

DHCP is responsible for giving / handing out the IP addresses for clients and servers which have sent out a DHCP request. It is not so crucial for Configuration Manager itself, but it's used in OS-deployment scenarios.

However, it is important to note how OS deployment works in Configuration Manager because it leverages PXE. PXE itself is an old piece of technology, has been around for ages, and is included as a part of the **WDS** (**Windows Deployment Services**) role of Windows Server. So, when we need to set up PXE in Configuration Manager, we have to enable a distribution point as PXE based.

When we want to deploy OS to a new client, it needs to start from PXE. If a client has PXE-enabled NIC, it will send out a DHCP request to its subnet, and it will only get a response from servers which have options 66 and 67 enabled (unless you have DHCP and WDS installed on the same server). When it has an IP address from DHCP, it will continue with a TFTP connection with the distribution point.

In many cases you might not have a DHCP server available in, for instance, a branch office or for other subnets (as DHCP is broadcast only, it will not go across multiple subnets). In this case, you might use IP helpers (cisco name for it) on switches and routers, or you can use DHCP relay which allows you to send DHCP packets across to other subnets.

Microsoft introduces a new feature in Windows Server 2012 which allows us to set up DHCP in a failover with multiple setup options.

In order to set up this solution, we need two active DHCP servers who are authorized in the domain.

And we have to create a scope in one of the DHCP servers; after that we can right-click on the scope and choose **Configure Failover...**, as you can see in the following screenshot:

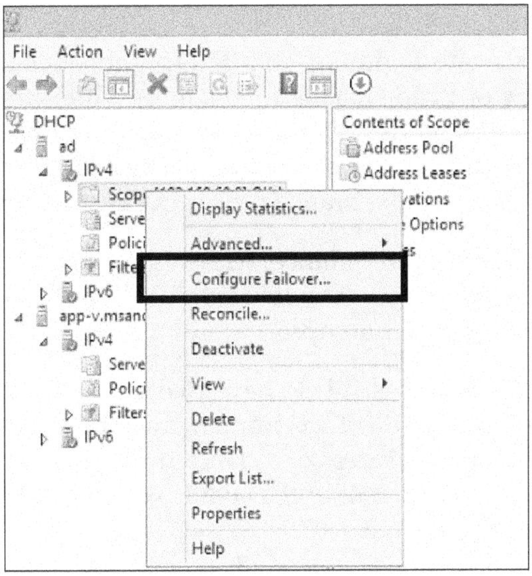

Here, we first have to add a partner server, and then choose what type of failover we want for the DHCP service:

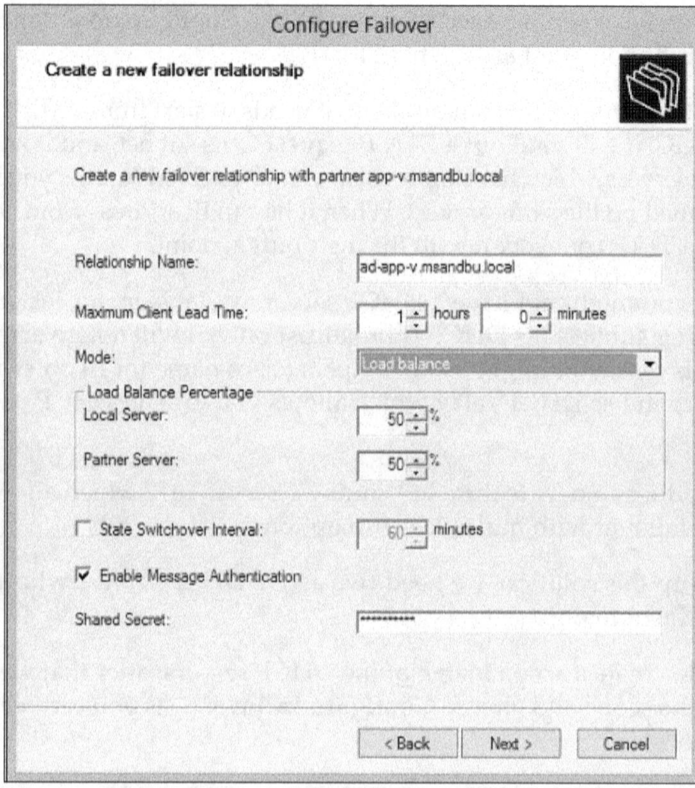

Here, we have different ways to deploy DHCP as highly available; either we can choose the **Hot standby** or **Load sharing** mode. In the **Hot standby** mode, one of the servers will stay in standby mode and take over if the primary server stops. This is primarily useful with branch offices and primary sites, where the primary DHCP server can take over scopes for the branch offices in case of failures.

The other option we have is **Load balance**, which is the default deployment mode. With this option, we have two servers who serve IP addresses and options to clients on a scope; this is an active-active setup.

The way in which DHCP server is able to have two separate DHCP servers running on the same subnet, is that Microsoft has implemented a hashing algorithm which calculates the hash of the Mac address of a client. If we have set up the percentage to be 50:50 for 10.0.0.0/24 scope, half of the clients will get an IP from within 10.0.0.1 - 128 range and rest from the 10.0.0.129 - 254 range.

DHCP also does a periodic rebalance check every five minutes to check that the load is correct; if one of the servers has eight clients and the other has four, it will do a rebalance since the ratio is 50:50, and move two of the clients to another server.

When one of the servers goes down in the failover scope, the remaining DHCP servers will stop using the hash algorithm and behave like a regular DHCP server and answer all the different DHCP requests.

Active Directory Certificate Services

With Configuration Manager deployed for Internet-based clients, we need to have a PKI solution in place, where we need to have certificates deployed to clients and servers.

Many of the different site roles also require different certificates types, so we need certificates on both for mutual authentication.

The following are the server roles that might require a certificate in Configuration Manager depending on the configuration:

- Management point
- Distribution point
- Software Update point
- State Migration point
- Enrollment point
- Enrollment Proxy point
- Application Catalog Web Service point
- Application Catalog Website point

Active Directory Certificate Services will be a crucial component and might be used a lot in other of the system center products as well.

The deployment of certificate services may vary depending on the size of the customer and what kind of security requirements they have.

It is important to note that Configuration Manager deployment requires the use of an Enterprise Root Certificate authority because of the requirements to edit templates in order to issue certificates to different servers.

The different templates and how to configure them can be found on TechNet from `http://technet.microsoft.com/en-us/library/gg699362.aspx`.

In many cases, a common scenario is having a two-tier-based PKI solution where we have an Offline Root Enterprise CA and an issuing subordinate CA, where the subordinate CA will issue certificates to the clients and servers with the approval of the Root CA.

In the following diagram we can see an example design on how a solution like this might look:

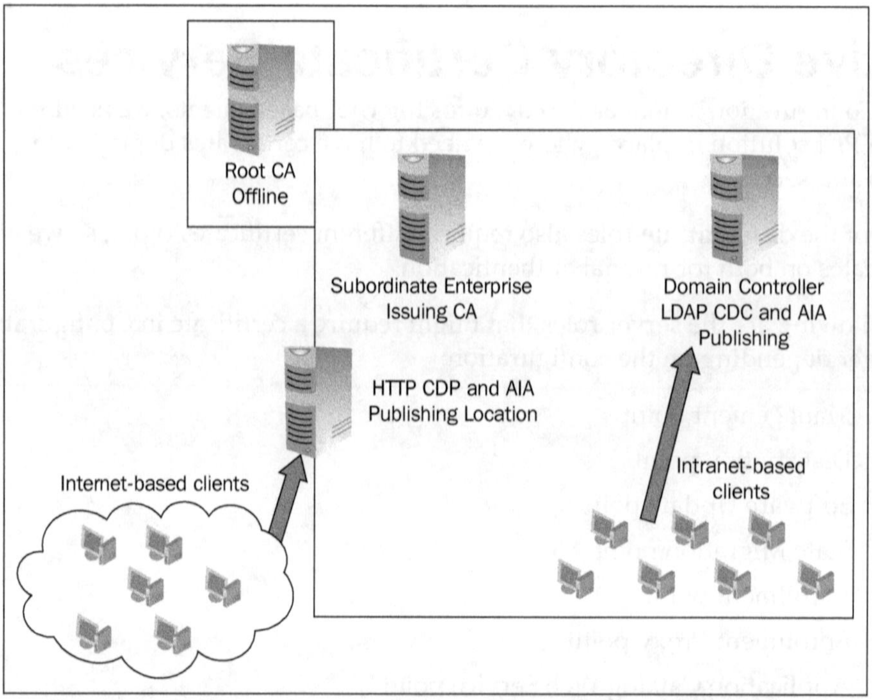

Also, we need to carefully plan where the base and delta **CRL (Certificate Revocation List)** is published out to the clients.

CRL is a list of certificates that have been revoked or that has been put on hold and therefore should no longer be trusted.

Same goes for **AIA** (**Authority Information Access**) location, which also should be accessible for clients so that they can get a copy of the issuing CA certificate in order to validate the certificate signature and to build a path to a trusted certificate. The CRL and AIA can be placed on different locations (URL, LDAP, or file share). As Configuration Manager will most likely contain a mix of Internet-based clients and intranet-based clients, it is always recommended to place the HTTP first on the CDP points to avoid network timeouts for the clients.

Both of these roles and features can be published and be available on web servers and can therefore be load balanced using Netscaler or the regular NLB features.

If we do not deploy these lists (CRLs) and roles (AIA) as highly available, and they go offline, clients might have trouble to verify the certificate chain depending on what policy has been set on the clients.

When setting up the subordinate CA, we have the option to deploy it as a failover cluster with an active/passive configuration. Because this in most cases will be the issuing CA, it should be set up as highly available.

In order to set up this cluster, there are a couple of prerequisites that need to be configured before we can deploy it.

We need to have two servers which have some form of shared attached storage (iSCSI or FC) before we can set up the failover cluster.

After that is done, we can set up the cluster accordingly to the previous cluster setup we did with SQL except instead of the file share witness; we add the disk-based addition to the cluster. After this, we need to run the cluster validation wizard and make sure that the cluster is set up properly.

After this is in place, we can start installing Active Directory on the first node of the cluster. Make sure that this node is the owner of the shared disk and has it mapped up to `E:\`.

> How to publish the CRL and AIA will not be covered in this chapter. The Configuration Manager team has created a how-to which can be found at `http://blogs.technet.com/b/configmgrteam/archive/2009/05/01/how-to-publish-the-crl-on-a-separate-web-server.aspx`.

As shown in the following screenshot, start by adding Active Directory **Certificate Authority** role on the owner of the shared node. This can be done from **Server Manager**. After the installation is done, we have to run the **Configure Active Directory Certificate Services on the destination Server** option; here we have to configure what kind of CA we want this node to be and where to store the certificate. So, first we choose to configure the CA.

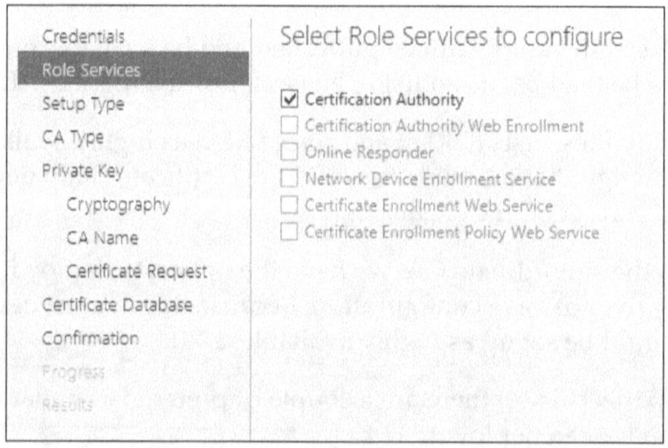

Next, we need to choose it as **Enterprise CA**:

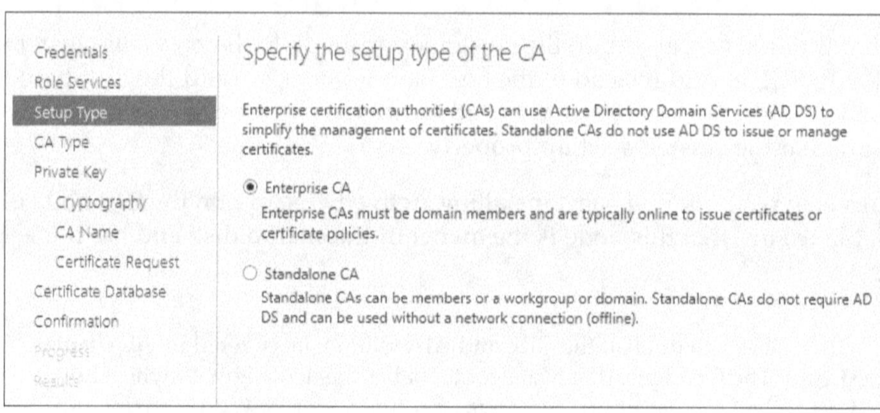

As we already have a Root CA in place, we need to define this as a subordinate CA.

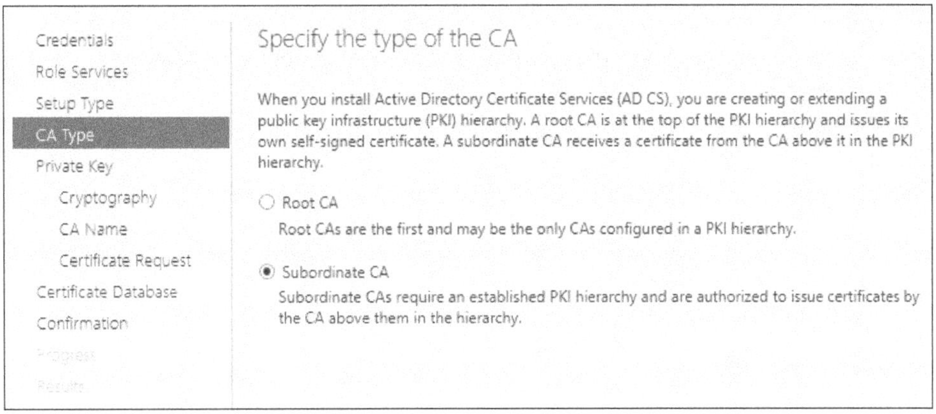

And because this is the first node, we need to create a new private key to use with the creation of the CA certificate using the option **Private Key**, as shown in the following screenshot:

> This procedure will not be needed on the second node because it will share the CA certificate.

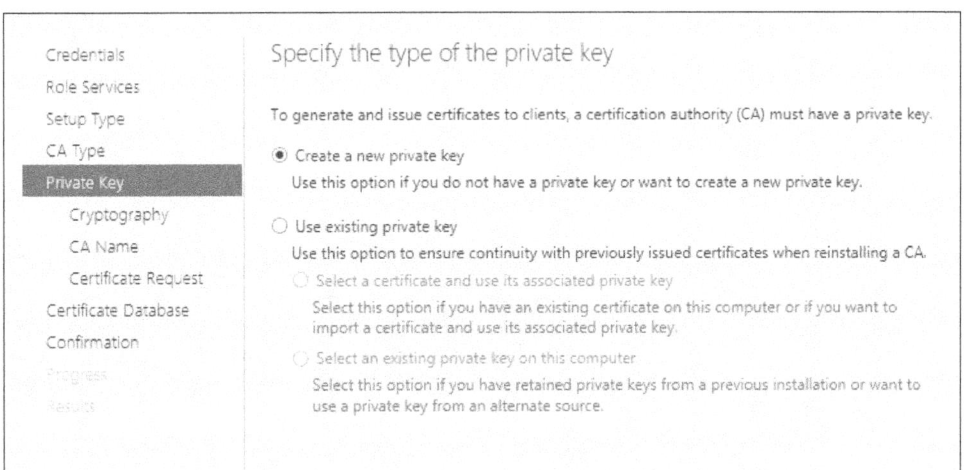

Now, choose what kind of encryption level we wish to use within the certificate, the default is 2048-bits. After that is done, we have to enter the value in **Common name for this CA**, as shown in the following screenshot. This is going to be the cluster role name, so we have to use the name we enter here again when we set up the cluster role.

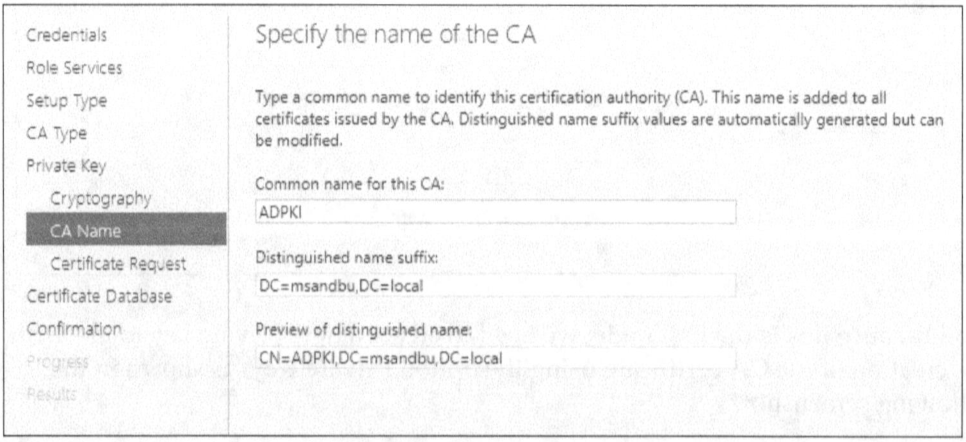

Next, we need to save the CA certificate request file to a disk, export it a remove drive like a USB stick, and import to the Root CA (if the subordinate CA does not get a certificate from the Root CA, the service will not start).

Now, under the **Certificate Database** location, we need to place this on the shared disk so that the cluster nodes have access to the database.

In my case, I have a shared disk mapped under `E:\`, as you can see in the following screenshot:

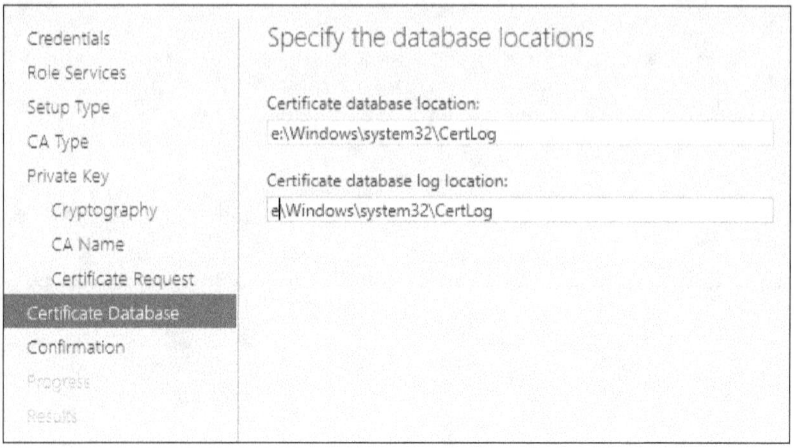

After that is done, we have to go to the Root CA and submit the request.

Open the **Certification Authority** console on the Root CA and choose **Submit new request** and browse for the newly created request file. After this, we need to choose a location where to place it:

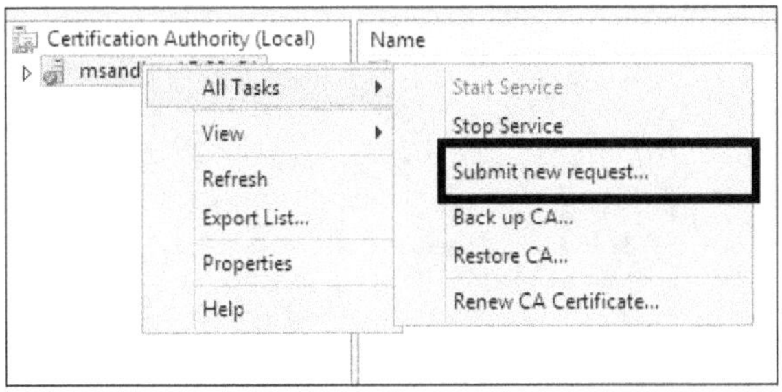

Now, go back to the cluster node we created the request file on. In the CA console, choose **Install CA Certificate...** as shown in the following screenshot. After this is done, we can start the service to make sure everything is functional.

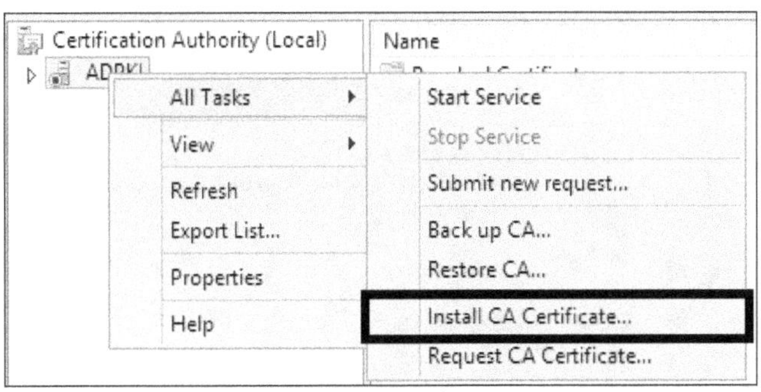

After we verify that the service is functional, we can continue with the second cluster node. First, we need to stop the CA service running on the first node, and move the cluster resources to the second cluster node. We also need to export the CA certificate from the first node with the private key to the second node; this can be done by navigating to the **Certificate Authority** console and choosing **Back up CA....**

> Make sure that the disk is attached to the second node before continuing on with the installation; you can see who the owner of the cluster disk is from **Failover Cluster Manager**.

Install the certificate authority on the second node, like we did with the first one. When we come to the **Private Key** settings, choose **Use existing private key**:

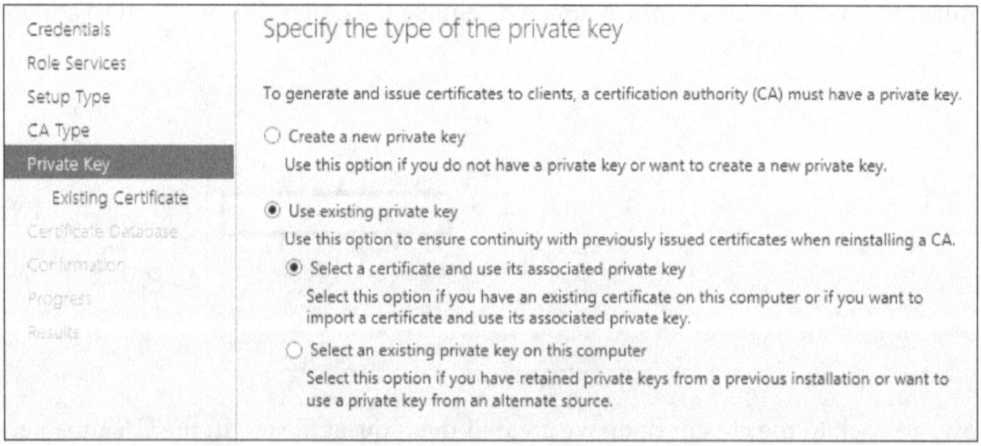

Now we need to choose **Import...** and then **Browse...** for the existing certificate that we exported previously:

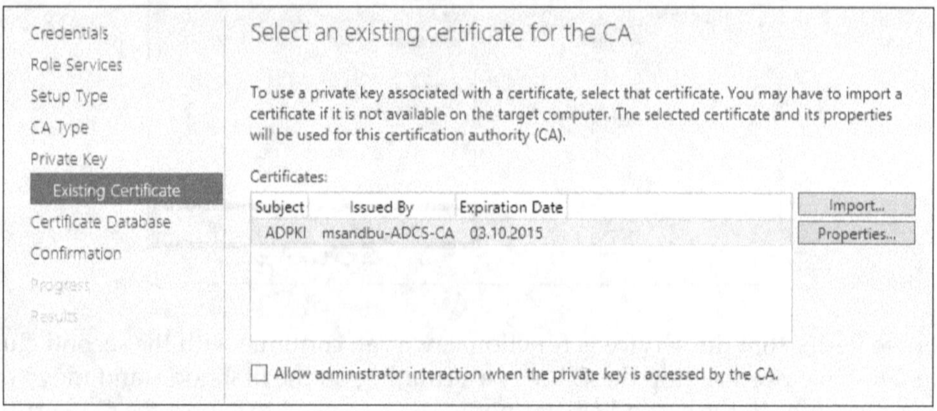

Next, we need to choose a location for the certificate database; this is going to be the same location as the previous node was set up with. You will get an error message saying that an existing database was found. Choose the option to overwrite it as shown in the following screenshot:

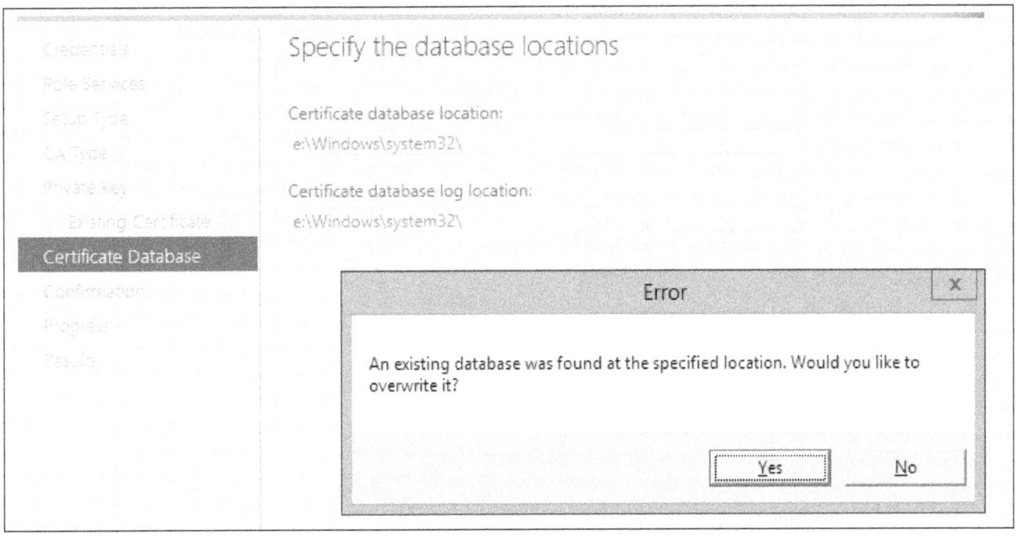

After this is done, we can finish up the CA installation on the cluster node. Start the CA service from the **Certification Authority** console and verify that the service is functional.

After we are done with that, we have to configure the CA role within the cluster. This is controlled by the CA service, the CA certificate, and the registry settings located under `SYSTEM\CurrentControlSet\Services\CertSvc`.

In **Failover Cluster Manager** (on the owner node of the cluster), right-click on the cluster and choose **Configure Role** and then choose **Generic Service** from the list, as shown in the following screenshot:

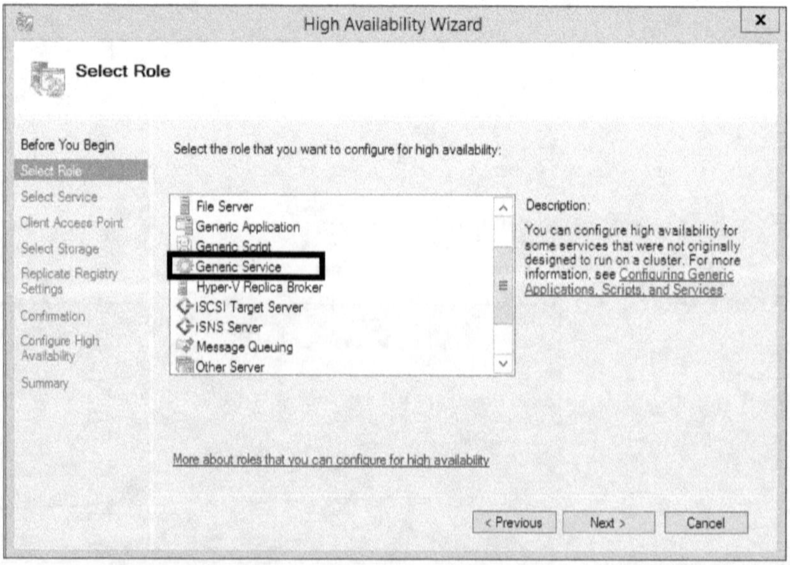

Next, we need to choose the **Active Directory Certificate Authority Services** option from the list, as shown in the following screenshot. This will allow the cluster to manage the service and will by default stop the service on the passive node. In case of failover, the cluster will start the service on the new owner node.

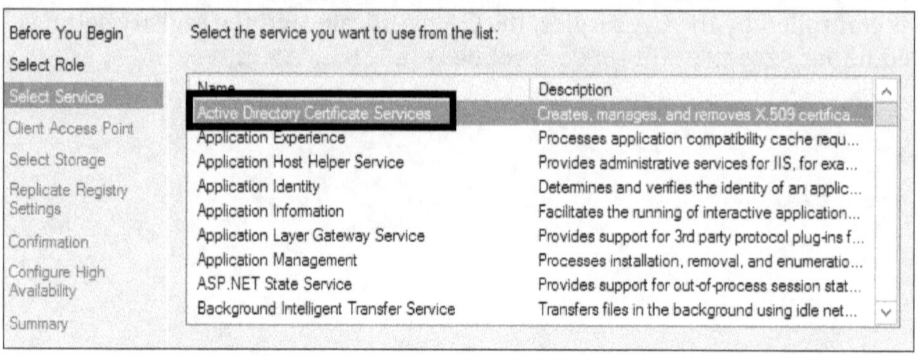

Under **Client Access Point**, we have to define the same common name we used earlier when we configured the certificate authority role. We also need to enter an IP address. Make sure that you are logged in as an enterprise admin user so that the cluster can create the specific objects within Active Directory as well as DNS.

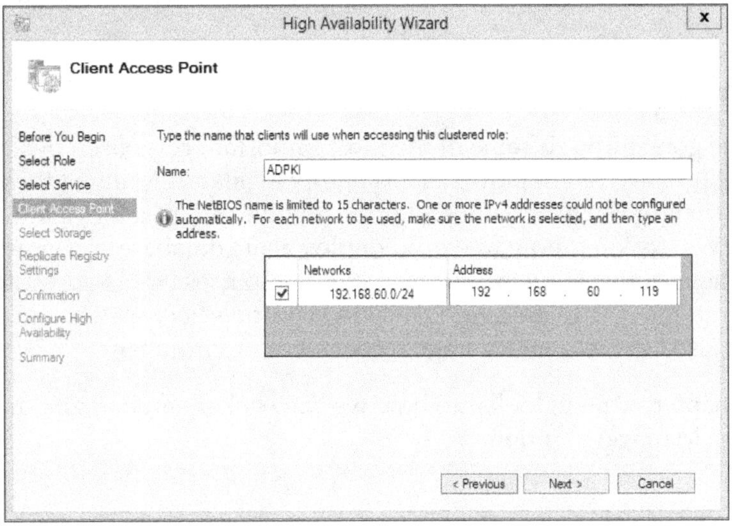

We can skip the storage part until after we have set up the cluster role.

There are also some registry settings we need to replicate between the hosts. This path contains most of the configuration of the certification service. So, enter the path `SYSTEM\CurrentControlSet\Services\CertSvc`, as shown in the following screenshot:

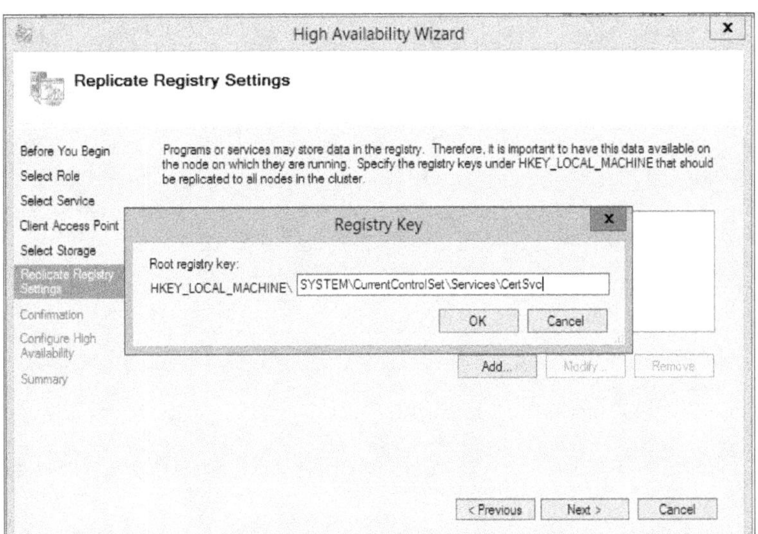

After this, we are done with the setup for the role service. The last part is that we need to add the shared storage to the cluster role; right-click on the role and choose **Add storage** and choose the cluster disk.

This binds the disk to the role and will follow the role on which its node is.

Summary

Now we have gone through some of the most important roles used by Configuration Manager and how we can deploy them as highly available. Many of these roles can be complex in a large environment and often involve other factors that we can cover in this book. We explored how we could deploy a site database server as a clustered SQL server, how Active Directory works, and how it uses DNS to operate. We also took a look into the new features of DHCP in Windows Server 2012 and failover options, and also how we can leverage these in our environment.

In the next chapter, we will look into how we can back up and restore our Configuration Manager solution.

4
Backup and Recovery

So far we have explored how we can set up Configuration Manager and the backend services as highly available, but it does not replace the need for backup. The need for backup will always be there in case of hardware failures and to avoid data loss. There are different components that we need to take backup of. In this chapter, we will cover topics such as:

- Backup up a site server
- Backup up content and packages in a Configuration Manager site
- Other components we need to think of
- Recovery

Backing up the site server

The first thing we will start with is backing up the site server; this task will take backup of the site database and site server configuration. This job can be set up as a scheduled task from within Configuration Manager. However, note that this does not take backup of the content but the site database alone.

[This task works only on the CAS and on primary sites. Secondary sites' data are stored in the primary site and do not need to be taken backup of separately.]

Go to **Administration** | **Sites** and right-click on the site you want, and choose **Site Maintenance** as shown in the following screenshot:

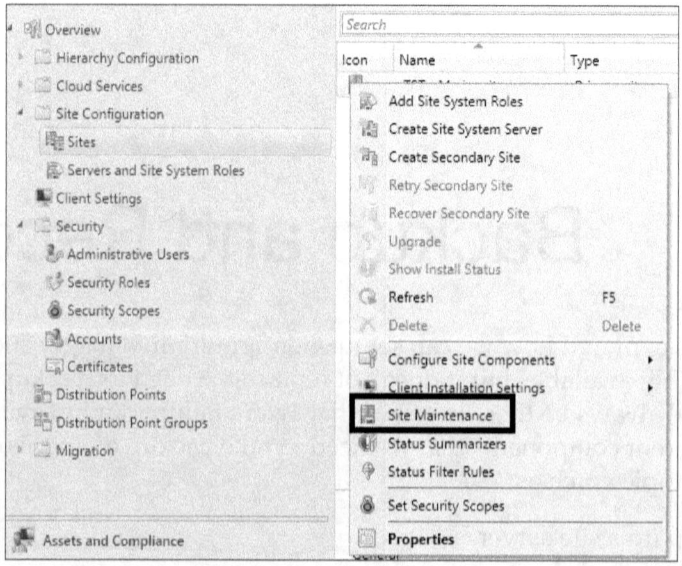

Choose **Backup Site Server Task** and select **Edit** as shown in the following screenshot.

There you can define a schedule for the task and define a backup location. This should be a network location, which should be a dedicated backup site. Depending on the business requirements, this should at least be done twice a week.

> You can also take a backup of the site database by using a maintenance plan from within SQL Server. This is an addition to the regular site server backup task, and the backup task within Configuration Manager is the recommended solution for taking full backup.

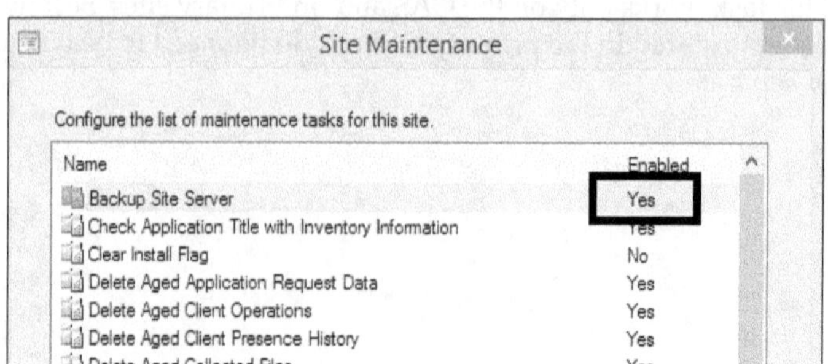

It is important to note that site server and the SQL Servers needs to have write NTFS rights and should share permissions to the `UNC` folder if this option is chosen.

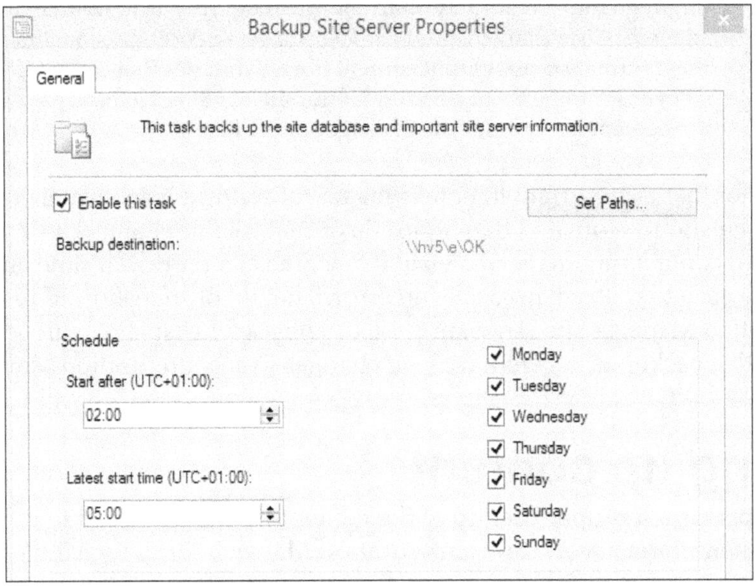

When you have defined a schedule and it has been run, you can review the backup successfully by checking the **Component Status** node in the **Monitoring** workspace. Review the status messages for **SMS_SITE_BACKUP**. When site backup is completed successfully, you see message ID 5035, which indicates that the site backup was completed without any errors. Or the Smsbkup.log

If we wish to trigger a backup manually, we can start the service **SMS_SITE_BACKUP** on the site servers from `services.msc`; this will run with the same parameters we defined within the task.

After the backup task is complete, the task tries by default to run the file `AfterBackup.bat`. This file is not there by default, and needs to be created and placed within the <ConfigMgrInstallationFolder>\Inboxes\Smsbkup folder. Within this `.bat` file we can define different scripts for archiving and to perform other tasks which are not part of the backup site server task.

> There is a known bug that might occur when restoring a site from a Configuration Manager 2012 Service Pack 1 backup and the database might go into a read-only state and the fix for this is to update the site with Cumulative Update 3. The site backup database includes the information about that content library, but not that content itself, so in order to perform a restore of the site content, we need to restore the content library and the package source files.

Another factor that is important to note is the use of snapshots in virtual environments. Many use snapshots before and then upgrade or make some changes on a virtual machine, as it contains an image of a virtual machine at a particular time and date, and makes it easy to rollback in case of an error. The use of snapshots to restore a Configuration Manager site is not supported. The use of snapshots can be used together with a backup task before making changes to a Configuration Manager server.

Backing up content

In order to perform a proper backup of the content library, we need to understand how the content library works in Configuration Manager 2012, which has been completely changed since 2007.

As shown in the following diagram, the content library is under the folder `SCCMcontentlib` (this folder is created on the disk with the most free space during setup):

> If we want to move the content library from one drive to another, we can use the `ContentLibraryTransfer.exe` tool, which can be found on the toolkit for Configuration Manager Service Pack 1.

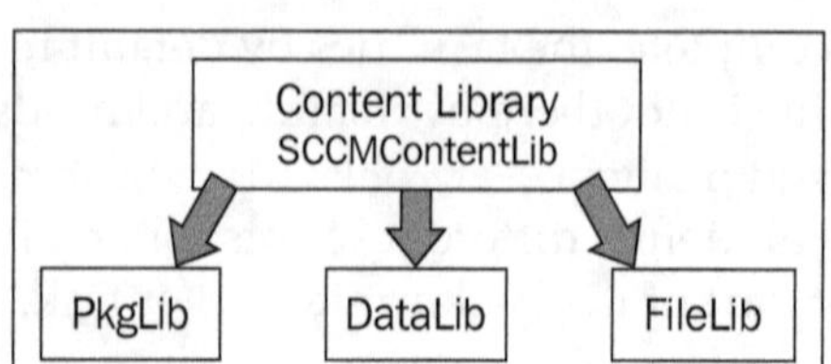

The content library consist of three folders: `PkgLib`, `DataLib`, and `FileLib`.

We have the `PkgLib` folder which contains a `.ini` file created with the ID name for each package. Each of the `.ini` file also contains a content ID to reference the data.

Then we have the `DataLib` folder, this contains a `.ini` file for each package and a folder for each package which contains each file in the source folder, these are just the signature hash files and not the real files. If we open a `.ini` file for a file in the `DataLib` folder, we can see a hash value for the file; the first four digits here are used under the `FileLib` folder.

Finally, we have the `FileLib` folder, which contains the actual files. Each file is stored in its own folder which contains the first four digits from the hash value of it. When we open the folder, we actually have file without an extension and the filename is the hash value of the file. So let's take an example package as shown in the following diagram:

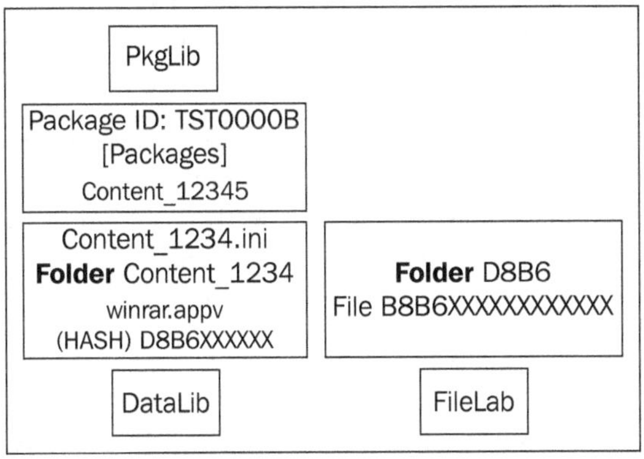

The following is the explanation of the components in the preceding example package:

- We have a package with ID **TST0000B** which is stored under the `PkgLib` folder with a `.ini` file that references it
- The `.ini` file of the package points to a content ID number, in this instance, **12345**
- Under the `DataLib` folder we have a `contentID.ini` file and a folder which uses the same ID file. In this folder, we have a copy of `winrar.appv` as a `.ini` file and within it, it has the hash value of the `winrar.appv` file
- Under the `FileLib` folder we have the the first four digits of the hash value referenced in a folder, and within that folder we can find the original file without a file extension

The site content library needs to be restored before we can redistribute content out to the distribution points in case of a failure. If not, we need to recreate the packages manually and distribute the content again.

A good way to take regular backup of this folder is either by using data protection manager or by using robocopy.

`robocopy` is a built-in file tool in Windows. We can use this for more granular file management and logging and to set up a built-in task to do a nightly backup of the content library.

A simple way to set it up is by using the command `robocopy C:\sccmcontentlib \\server\ %date:~-4,4%%date:~-10,2%%date:~7,2% /LOG:\\backupserver\logs\log.txt`. It will make a copy of the folder and place it on a network share .

The parameters `%date:~-4,4%%date:~-10,2%%date:~7,2%` are used to create a new folder on the destination server which contains the date. This can be used to create a scheduled task which runs a backup once each week to a new folder each time with the date.

We also need to have a copy of the source files to the packages if we need want to be able to restore the content. If we are unsure where the source files might be, we can run a query against the SQL Server to locate the content. By running the query `Select * from v_package`, we can list out all the packages and where the source fields are located, as shown in the following screenshot:

	PackageID	Name	P...	PkgSourcePath
1	TST00001	User State Migration Tool for Windows 8	2	C:\Program Files (x86)\Windows Kits\8.1\Assessment and ...
2	TST00002	Boot image (x86)	2	\\SCCM.msandbu.local\SMS_TST\osd\boot\i386\boot.T...
3	TST00003	Configuration Manager Client Package	2	\\SCCM.msandbu.local\SMS_TST\Client
4	TST00004	Configuration Manager Client Upgrade Package	2	\\SCCM.msandbu.local\SMS_TST\ClientUpgrade
5	TST00005	Boot image (x64)	2	\\SCCM.msandbu.local\SMS_TST\osd\boot\x64\boot.T...
6	TST00006	Windows 8.1	2	\\hv5\G\sources\install.wim
7	TST00007	Task Sequence 2	1	
8	TST00008	boot	2	\\sccm\SMS_SITE\boot.TST00008.wim

In many cases, these source files might be located on a SAN solution and should also be taken backup of.

When restoring a site with its source and content, perform the following steps:

1. Restore the source files to its content.
2. Restore the site content library.
3. Restore the site database (since it is the database that references all the different content libraries and package sources; the other two steps need to be taken care of before we do a site restore).

Backing up user state migration data

The site backup maintenance task does not take backup of the state migration folders which are placed on state migration servers. These folders should also be taken backup of in case of disaster.

Backing up custom reports

If we are creating custom reports, we should take backup of these as well because they are not covered by the site backup maintance task. The information on how to back up a reporting services instance with custom reports can be found at `http://technet.microsoft.com/en-us/library/ms155814.aspx`.

> When we upgrade our Configuration Manager site, the predefined reports are overwritten by new ones. To make sure that we have altered a predefined report, we take backup of these reports.

Backing up a cloud-based distribution point

When setting up a cloud-based distribution point, we need to install a management certificate in order to allow it to authenticate and encrypt traffic going to Microsoft Azure. This certificate also needs to be backed up, as it allows our site server to communicate with the roles in Azure. This certificate needs to be taken backup of. A certificate does not change that often (depending on the expiration date), we only need to take backup of it once. This can be done via the **MMC** console and certificate snap-in. Right-click on the certificate and choose **Export...** as shown in the following screenshot. It is also important that we choose to export the certificate with the private key.

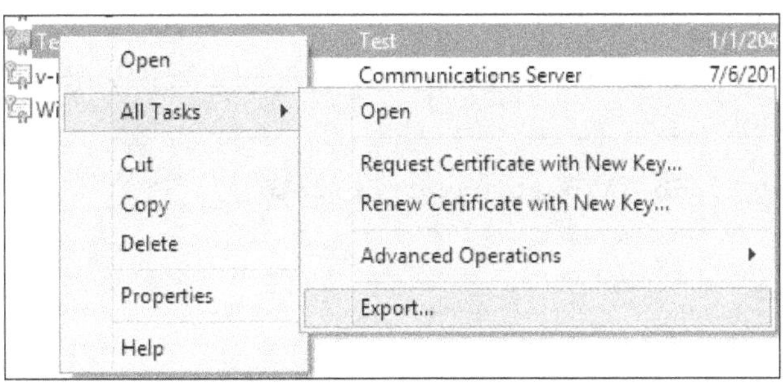

Backing up the Certification Authority

It is very important to take the backup of the CA we have. Even if we have it deployed in a cluster, we still need to take its backup in case of a disaster. The components we need to take backup of the CA are:

- The CA certificate
- The configuration files
- The database

The CA certificate can be taken backup of by using the command-line tool `certutil`. To do this, we need the following parameters:

```
certutil -backup -ppasswordc:\backup
```

> Here the password is a password for the private key.

The configuration files are stored in registry and can be taken backup of by using the command `reg export`; this does an export of the registry settings contained in a registry hive into a simple `.reg` file.

We can use it with the following parameters to take backup of the configuration into a `.reg` file called `regkey.reg`:

```
 reg export HKLM\System\CurrentControlSet\Services\CertSvc\
Configurationc:\backup\regkey.reg
```

It is also important to note that a system state backup using the internal Windows Backup tool also backs up the registry hive and the whole certificate services' role configuration.

To back up the CA database, we can use the `certutil` tool, with the following parameters:

```
certutil.exe -backupdb \\locationserver\folder
```

Restoring a site server

What if something catastrophic happens and our solution goes down and we need to restore? In order to restore a site server, we need to at least have a backup first (either if it is the database or a complete backup set). If we have a backup media in place, we can run the Configuration Manager setup from the installation media:

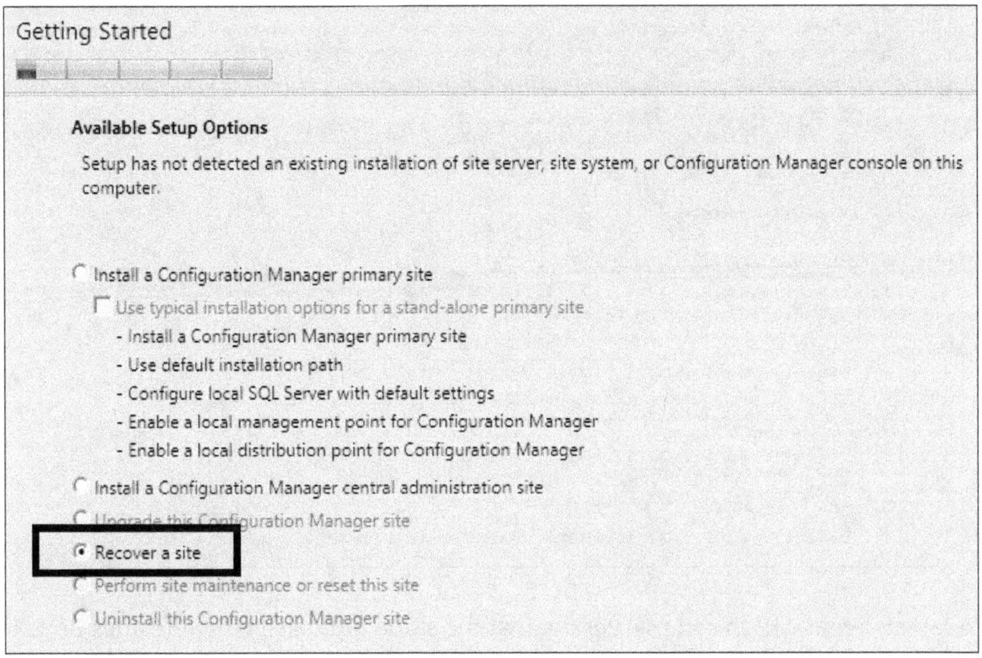

Now when we choose **Recover a site**, we have different options. We can, for instance, choose **Restore using an existing backup set**.

> This option cannot be chosen if there is a site installation already in place on the computer.

We can recover the site from an existing database backup (this can be chosen if you already have a site server installed), as shown in the following screenshot. This performs a database restore from the backup media.

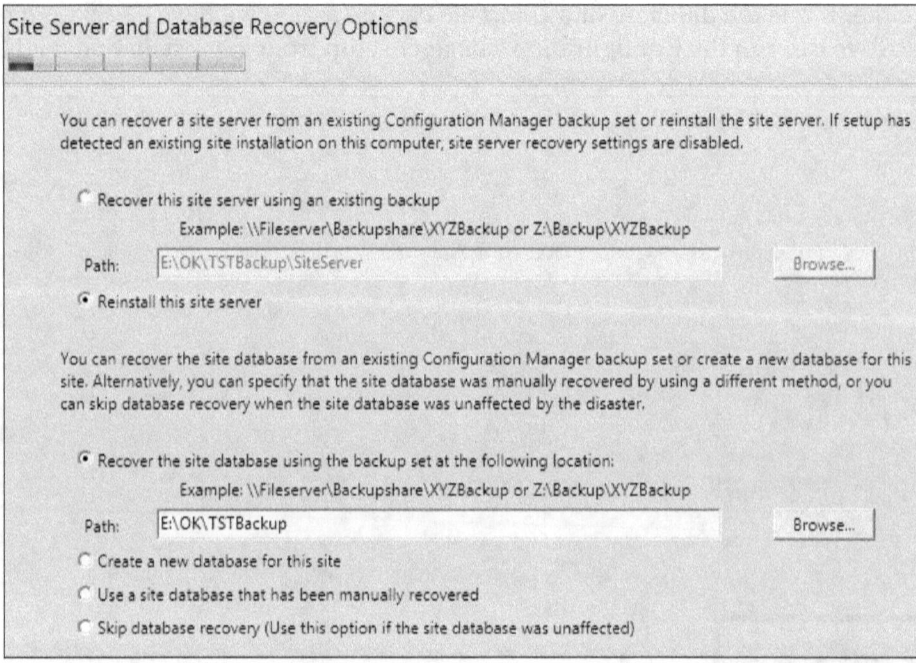

We can also reinstall the site server against the same database which resides on the SQL Server. Note that this requires you to use the same site code and the same database name when reinstalling.

> After we have reinstalled a site server, we need to reinstall any hotfixes that were installed to the site server, we also need to renter any user account password as they are reset when we perform a restore.
> All procedures that need to be done after a recovery are stored in the `C:\ConfigMgrPostRecoveryActions.html` file on the site server.

Restoring a secondary site server

As we cannot back up a secondary site, we need to recover a secondary site from a primary site. We can restore a secondary server from the **Configuration Manager** console. Right-click on the secondary site in **Configuration Manager** and choose **Recover secondary site**. Remember that there are a few of prerequisites that need to be in place in order to perform a successful restore:

- The server to which we want to restore the secondary site server needs to have the same FQDN as the old server.
- It needs to have the same security rights as the old server.
- It should use the same installation path as the old server used.
- It needs to have SQL Express installed before recovering. The SQL Express version needs to be the same as it was before and should have the same instance.

Summary

Now we have looked through many of the different components that need to be taken backup of. We looked into the specific Configuration Manager components that we can take backup of and how we can restore them.

As I mentioned before, it is important to remember that high availability is not an alternative to backup. Even if you implement high availability, you should always have a backup in place.

In the next chapter, we will take a look at how we can fine tune the performance of different components within Configuration Manager because it uses a lot of different roles within Windows Server that can be adjusted for better use.

5
Performance Tuning

So far we have gone through different scenarios of high-availability as well as backup and restoring. In this last chapter we will focus on how we can tune our solution according to best practice to gain better performance. In many cases, there are also some settings or configurations that need some fine tuning.

Some of the topics we will go through in this chapter are:

- How to configure different roles according to best-practice
- Performance tuning for a Windows server
- Performance tuning for a SQL server
- Performance tuning for OS deployment
- Performance tuning for Configuration Manager

Servers

Before we go into the different server roles, we need to address the general hardware requirements when planning for server roles. Most of the roles (CAS, primary site, secondary site, and distribution points) in Configuration Manager need to have, at general, a minimum of four CPU cores and 8 GB of RAM, but there are some exceptions to this rule. For management points it follows the general requirement, it should have at least four cores and at least 8 GB of RAM. This role is more reliant on memory and processor capacity because it is handling much encrypted network traffic from the clients. For distribution points they should, in general, have at least two cores and 8 GB of RAM. This role is more reliant on network and disk I/O because it's used in OS and application deployments. So if you are setting this up as a virtual machine, remember that you should use synthetic adapters, since it supports 1 GBps interfaces.

You can read more about the hardware requirements on TechNet `http://technet.microsoft.com/en-us/library/hh846235.aspx`.

Another thing that should be taken into account is to have the latest Windows updates, both for Windows server and for System Center, as they might contain performance fixes as well as bugs and security patches.

> At the time of this writing, the latest patch for Configuration Manager was Service Pack 1 CU3, and when upgrading to CU3, some users experienced more bugs and instability and a postfix was deployed. So it is important not to install the newest patches immediately, but try to test them, if possible, or verify if other users have experienced issues with the latest patches. A great place to see if others are trying the latest patches is on the Configuration Manager forums, which can be found at `https://social.technet.microsoft.com/Forums/en-US/home?category=systemcenter2012configurationmanager`.

Also make sure that you have the latest drivers and firmware updates for the following:

- BIOS (if it is a physical server)
- SAN drivers (if you are using a SAN against a computer)
- NIC firmware (if it is a physical server)
- NIC drivers (if it is a physical server)
- Latest integration pack from virtualization hypervisor

The last point is important for virtual environments, since they contain new drivers for the virtual machines. If you are running Hyper-V 2012 and you have virtual machines running an older version of the operating system as a guest OS, you most likely need to upgrade the integration pack. This can be done from within hyper-v manager.

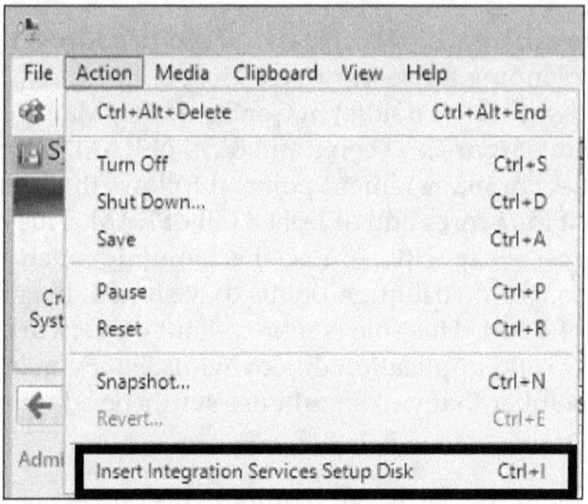

As a best practice, the integration services should be installed on our base image. Note that for Windows Server 2012, the integration service is already installed on the operating system.

Another thing is that 2008 R2 and 2012 servers have, by default, enabled a power state, called balanced, which conserves energy based on the utilization of the CPU, this can be altered by changing the power plan to High-performance.

As for physical servers, many have built-in power saving options in their BIOS and should be disabled if we are having performance issues on our physical hosts.

Since Configuration Manager is not supported to run on Windows server core, we need to do some fine-tuning ourselves. Most of the servers using 2008 or 2012 R2 versions contain a lot of services which are not often used or rarely used at all and can be disabled as well, such as:

- Themes service (controls the active theme and when you want to change themes)
- Print Spooler (controls connectivity to the printer and spools jobs to the printer)
- DHCP client (disabled when using static IP NB, and this service also handles dynamic updates)
- Network Location Awareness (used to locate what network the server sits on, can affect firewall policies which are set to domain profile)

In general, remember that you need to check the fragmentation level of the disks from time to time the servers are running on; since if a disk is highly fragmented, it takes the machine longer time to fetch the content and deliver it to the clients. This applies to both physical and virtual environments (this does not apply to SSD disks).

It is also important to note that Configuration Manager site server in general does a lot of read/write I/O to the disk. Therefore you should also look into using it, for instance **redundant array of independent disks** (**RAID**) or storage spaces (where they can be used), to improve the performance of the site server.

Also if we are having some trouble with performance on a site server collocated with roles, we should consider moving other roles on to dedicated servers as well.

Virtualizing hosts and physical servers

With Windows Server 2012, Microsoft also introduced NIC teaming as a new feature as a native feature on the OS (this is mostly for physical servers, since virtual servers NICs are protected by the hypervisor host, which in most cases have NIC teaming themselves). The advantages of using NIC teaming is that it allows for redundancy and load-balancing which gives us a better performance. NIC teaming can be setup by using Server Manager and going into the local server dashboard.

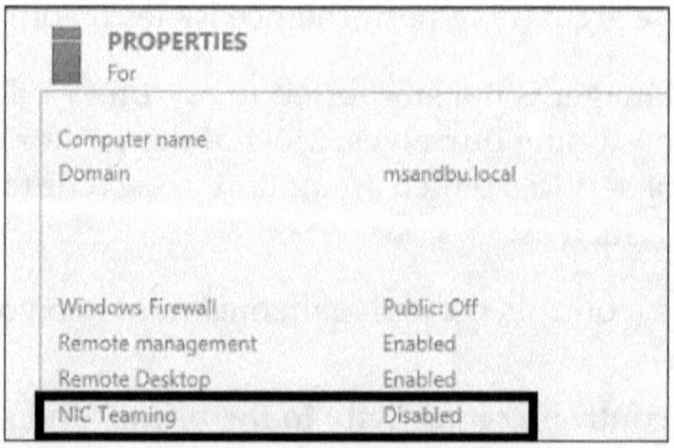

When setting up NIC teaming, we need to choose what NICs we want to add to the team and what kind of configuration we want. We have three kinds of teaming modes:

- **Static Team**
- **Switch Independent**
- **LACP** (Link Aggregation Control Protocol)

We also have different load balancing modes for each of the teaming modes. A static team means that you need to configure link aggregation on the switch before we setup the team. There we define which ports and what kind of VLANs can enter the virtual NIC. If we use LACP, the switch is configured with a number of ports enabled as LACP and then the switch and the server will automatically setup an automatic link with the VLANs. Both of these modes give us both better bandwidth and redundancy on the same switch in case of a NIC failure. By using the switch independent teaming, we can connect a server to multiple switches. This gives us redundancy (over multiple switches) and better performance from the server to the clients but not the other way since it is a team which is spread across different switches. This is because the ports are connected to two independent switches which have no knowledge that they have the same computer attached to one another.

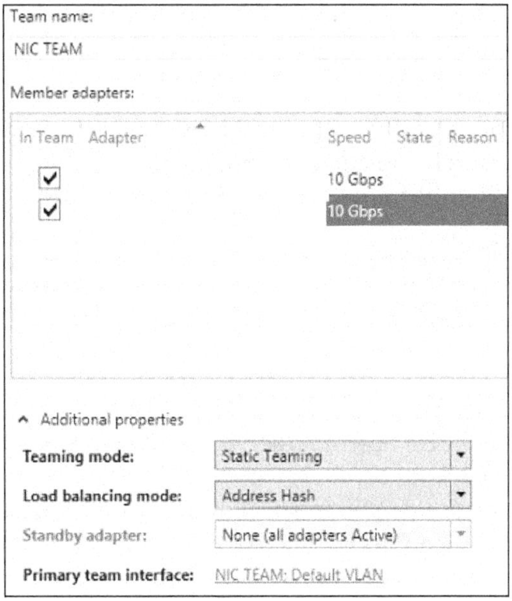

In some cases, with many servers and clients, it might have some difficulties negotiating speed and duplex with the switch port; this can be seen if you have a slow content transfer over a gigabit link. This can be changed from the network adapter driver.

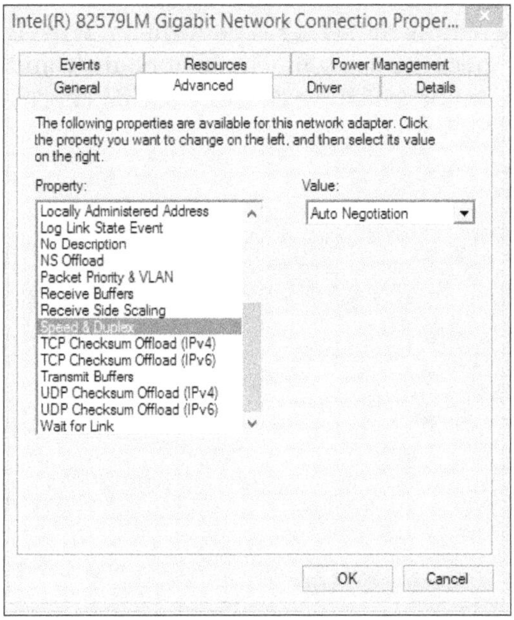

You can also use the following PowerShell command to get the same information:

```
Get-NetAdapterAdvancedProperty -Name Ethernet
```

Another feature that can be adjusted is Jumbo Frames, which allows sending larger frames over the network. This needs to be adjusted according to the rest of your network. Check what kind of frame size your network equipment supports.

Now most of the roles in Configuration Manager are based upon using HTTP; either it is client connectivity or content fetching. They use **Internet Information Services (IIS)** server and therefore, is important to understand how we can tune it accordingly.

In most cases, we will have encrypted network traffic coming from the clients to these web servers. This traffic, which is SSL-based, puts quite a strain on the CPU on the servers, since the CPUs need to decrypt all the content bit by bit. In *Chapter 3, Deploy Highly Available Backend Services*, we went through some of the options where we can put a network load balancer in front of the role (**Application Catalog** and **Application Catalog Service Point**), which can handle the SSL traffic and send decrypted traffic back to the web servers. This removes a lot of CPU cycles from the web server since it does not need to handle the encrypted traffic.

Identifying bottlenecks

It is important to know how to get the performance overview of the servers when we believe they are having some performance issues. By looking into task manager, it will give you the quick view of CPU, memory, and LAN usage which might give us a quick picture of how the server is performing. If we wish to get a better overview of what resources are using much memory, disk, and network I/O, we can go into performance monitor which we can access from task manager.

The screenshot of **Task Manager** view is as follows (with a shortcut to performance monitor):

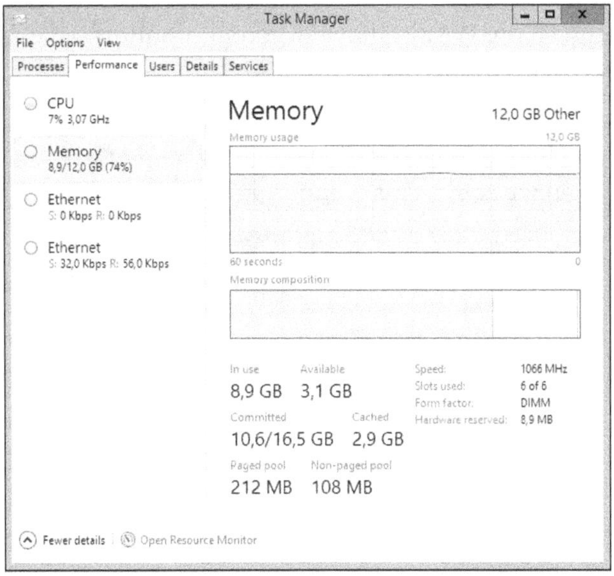

Resource Monitor gives us a deeper overview of what processes are using memory, CPU, disk I/O, and network I/O.

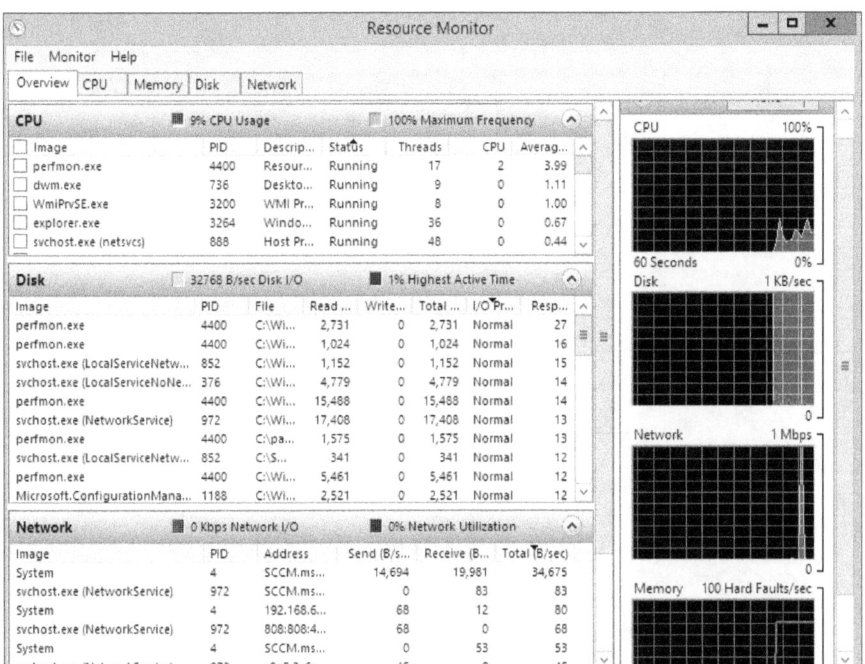

We can also use **Performance Monitor** to view the resource usage of different components within Configuration Manager. We have a lot of precreated monitors we can see for different components, for instance, MP, DP, PXE, Software metering, inventory status, and so on. We also have different monitors for checking out SQL performance on the SQL server.

Now if we open **Performance Monitor** on the site server, we can get out a lot of performance monitors related to it, for instance, how many DDR records are generated on the site server when we activate user and system discovery against AD.

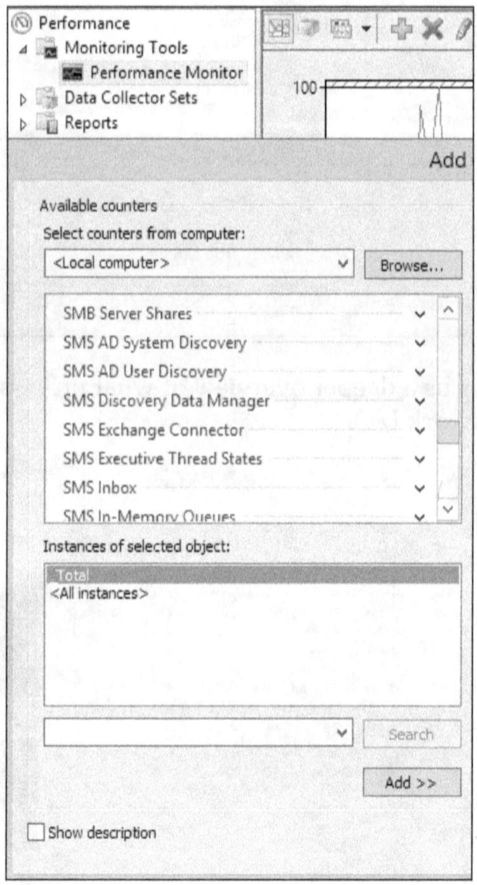

Microsoft has also created a tool called **Best Practices Analyzer** (**BPA**), which is part of Windows Server 2012. This tool scans a server according to different categories and checks if all the different Windows server features are set up according to the best practice. This tool is available within Server Manager.

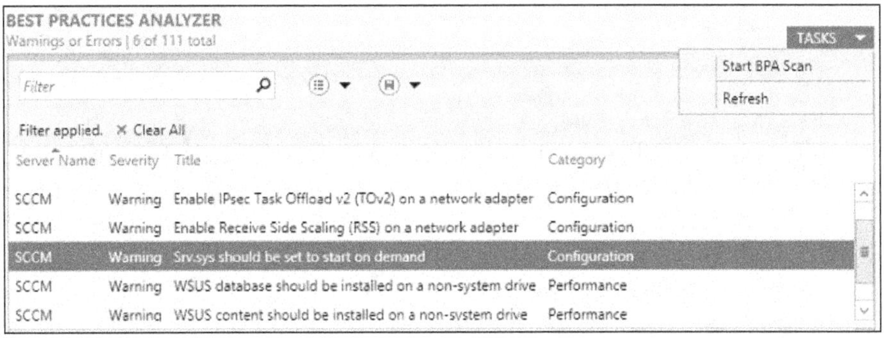

It gives you feedback based upon the Windows server features that are installed and gives you information on what you need to do; but it does not analyze any Configuration Manager roles. Thankfully, Microsoft has created its own tool for this, called Baseline Configuration Analyzer. You can download this tool from Microsoft download site: `http://www.microsoft.com/en-us/download/details.aspx?id=16475`. In order to use it against Configuration Manager, we also need to download the System Center 2012 SP1 Configuration Analyzer, which can be downloaded from `http://www.microsoft.com/en-us/download/details.aspx?id=36796`. This comes with a set of scripts and settings which are used to scan against all of the system center products to see if they are according to the best practice.

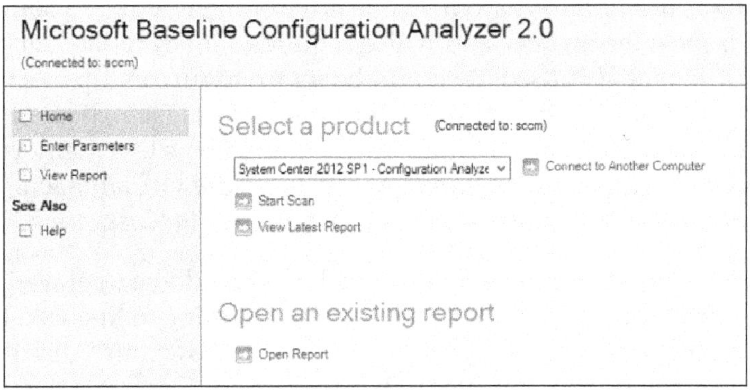

So after you have installed both the tools, all you have to do is choose a product and do a scan against a Configuration Manager server. Then it will run a number of scripts against the target host and generate a report, which will show what needs to be done and what is configured according to the best practice.

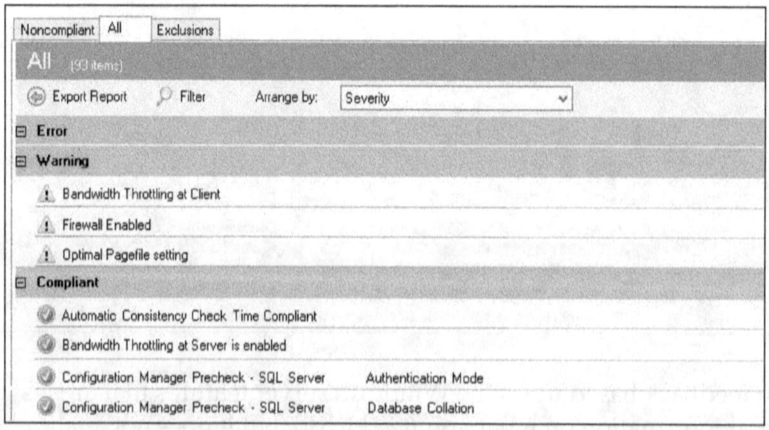

These add-ons tend to be updated for each release of System Center, so therefore, if we have an older version or a newer version then the add-ons will not work. So make sure that you have same version of the add-on as the system center product installed.

Virtualization hosts

Running Configuration Manager in a virtual environment will be a standard deployment for most businesses, and it also requires a lot of tuning for performance in most cases. If Hyper-V is used, it should be set up to run on top of a Server Core instance, since this removes the uneeded features, such as GUI, .NET, and file explorer. We can also use Server Hyper-V which consumes less memory and CPU cycles to the virtualization engine and leaves more to the virtual machines. This version can only be used for Hyper-V and can not have, for instance, GUI on top.

Setting up high I/O applications as virtual machines should be deployed with a fixed disk size, since this reduces the CPU overhead when writing to the disk. It is important to note that for using a fixed disk size, you need to plan how much disk space you need; also when using backup tools to backup a VM with fixed size, it needs to backup the empty blocks as well. We can also use VHDX format which is a new virtual disk format that came with Windows Server 2012. This new format is more resilient to corruption and uses a 4k block size and automatically aligns its disk partitions.

Usage of the snapshot feature in Hyper-V creates a differencing VHD disk. Having only a few snapshots will use more CPU cycles against the storage, so make sure that you have a short chain of snapshots.

Hyper-V also has a number of network offloading features which removes some of the CPU overhead. This includes:

- TCP/UDP checksum offloading
- Virtual machine queue (VMQ)
- Receive Side Scaling (RSS)
- Large send offload

These can be enabled under the network card configuration where we enabled Jumbo Frames earlier.

IIS

Now when we set up a server role in Configuration Manager, which uses IIS in the bottom, most of the cases, out of the box, set up for best performance; however there are some settings that can be fine-tuned.

We can define an alternate location for the IIS logfiles since they, by default, are created on the local server. You can change this by navigating to **IIS manager** | **Default web site** | **Logging**.

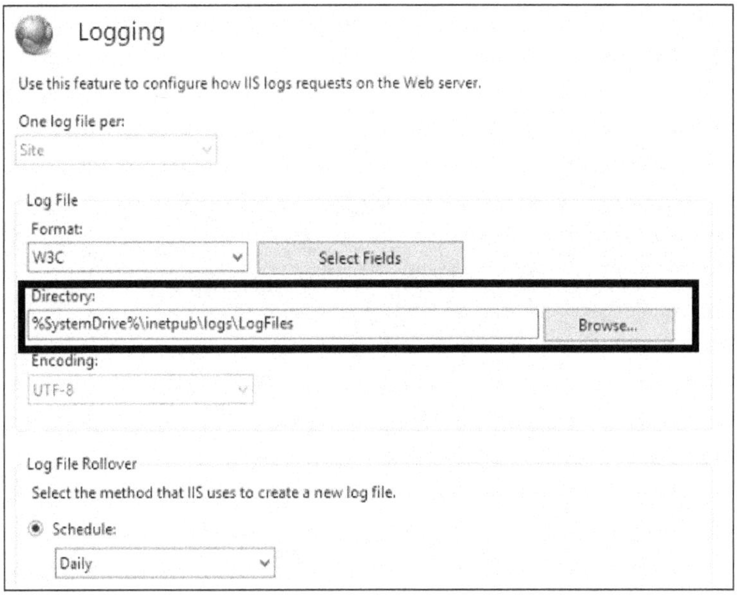

By placing this on a network location, we remove disk I/O and disk space from the local disk on the server. If you do not need to have logging enabled, you should disable this feature to reduce the I/O.

Another important thing to note is that, by default, application pools that are created in IIS by Configuration Manager are recycled in every 29 hours. So the first request that reaches IIS after the application pool is recycled will process very slowly because the application pool is set to work on demand. With Windows Server 2012 IIS, we have the option to define an application pool as **AlwaysRunning**, which will make request that are made after the application pool has recycled response faster. This setting can be altered by navigating to **IIS** | **Application Pool** | **Advanced Settings**.

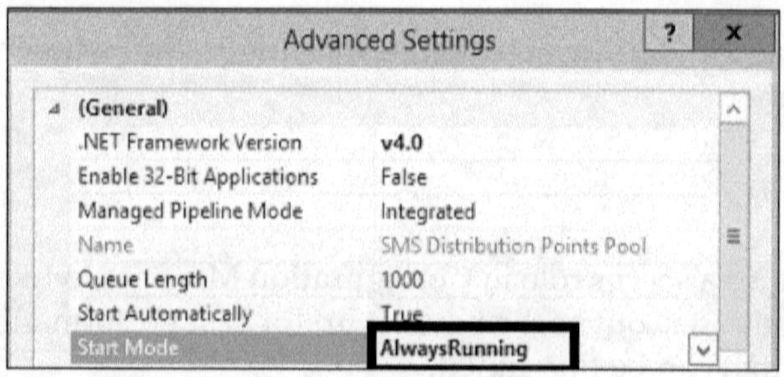

To enable a low form of bandwidth usage between clients and management points in Configuration Manager, we can use HTTP compression. This compresses all of the HTTP traffic between a client and a management point; but this comes at the cost of the CPU. In some cases, where you have sufficient bandwidth but getting too many CPU cycles, we can disable compression on the IIS server (this is enabled by default by Configuration Manager).

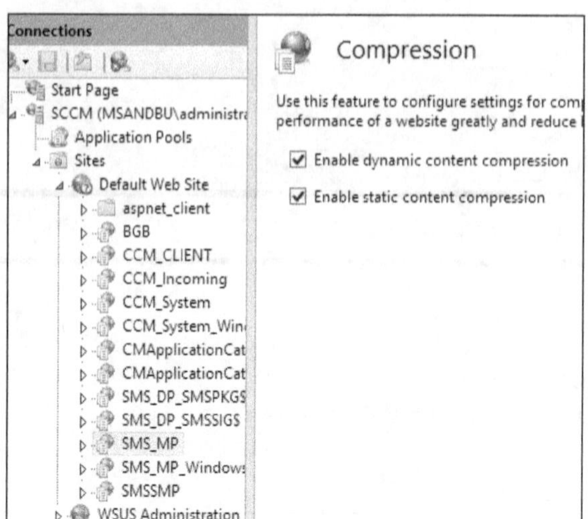

A SQL server

When setting up a SQL server, it is important to plan the hardware requirements accordingly.

SQL server is a disk I/O intensive role, like I mentioned in *Chapter 1, Planning for High Aailability with Configuration Manager*, we should split out the different databases and components into different disks which then has different levels of RAID for performance and redundancy to gain optimal performance. So make sure that the site database, tempdb, and the SQL logs are installed on different volumes. When we have set up a SQL server, it is important to note that the SQL role hogs as much memory as it can and can then potentially consume all of the memory on the server it is running on (especially, if it is running on a virtual server with dynamic memory enabled). Configuration Manager requires SQL server to reserve a minimum of 8 GB of memory in the buffer if it is used by an instance which is either a Central Administration site or a Primary site. So if we used a dedicated SQL instance, we need to limit the memory available for the SQL server to about 80 to 90 percent. This can be done via accessing the management console of SQL server. Navigate to **Server** | **Memory** | **Maximum server memory (in MB)** and adjust it to be around 80-90 percent.

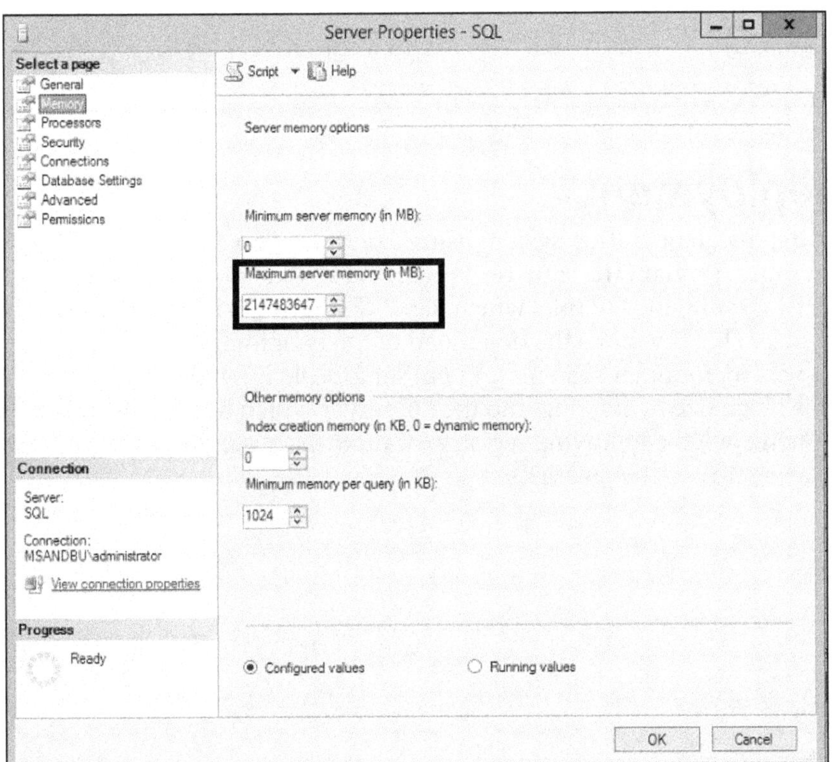

Also remember that you can use **Activity Monitor** to see if queries are using a lot of CPU time. This might be a good indicator that you are having performance issues on your SQL server. You can start activity monitor by starting Management Console. Right-click on the **MSSQL** instance and choose **Activity Monitor**. This gives us a good indicator on what type of queries are taking long time and using CPU on the SQL server.

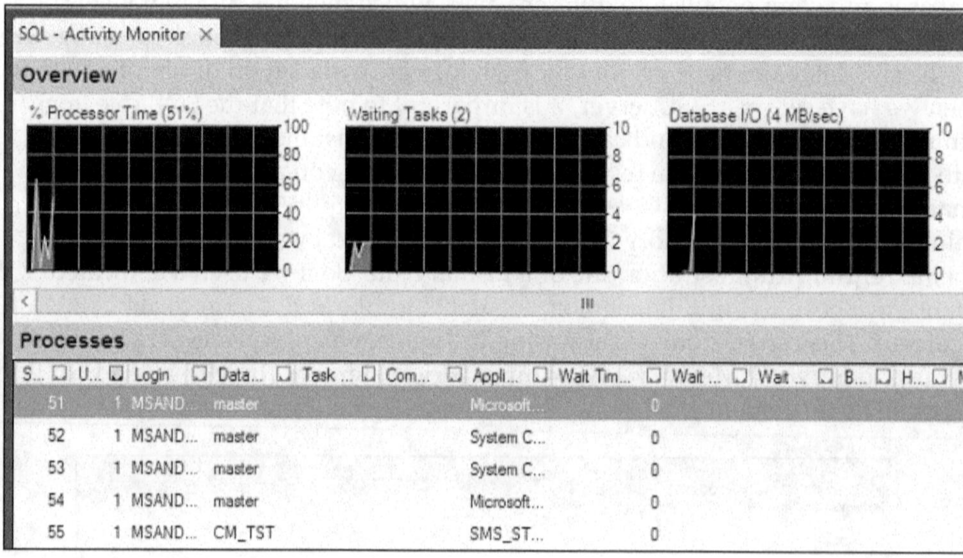

OS-deployment

When we deploy an operating system using Configuration Manager and WDS, it uses a protocol called **Trivial File Transfer Protocol (TFTP)** to download the content to the client. By default, the DP role, which has PXE and WDS installed, uses a fixed low block size. This can make the download of the boot image pretty slow, since the block size was set for older systems and not set to scale up to newer systems. You can change this block size by logging into the DP server which has PXE enabled, and start registry. Then open the following registry location: `HKEY_LOCAL_MACHINE\SOFTWARE\wow6432node\Microsoft\SMS\PXE`.

Then add the dWord key called `RamDiskTFTPBlockSize` and add the value to `16384`. This will make the PXE server operate with much larger blocks when sending content over TFTP. Another important feature is the ability to use multicast OS-based deployments, in contrast to the regular unicast traffic. The reason to use multicast is that multiple computers can receive from the same traffic stream (one to many) unlike regular unicast (one to one). This way you can distribute one deployment out to many computers at the same time. This requires that all computers need to start receiving at the same time, also it adjusts the traffic stream to accommodate the slowest endpoint subscribing to the stream of data. This way we can remove a lot of network traffic from the multicast server, since it only needs to send out one stream. Important thing to note is that using multicast is a good option if you have multiple computers that needs to be deployed at the same time. For one-to-one scenarios, multicast is a much slower option than using unicast. If you need a mass deployment of many computers simultaneously, which needs the same image, you should enable multicast. It is important to note that we need to have network equipment that supports multicast, and if we have older network equipment this might become an issue. Also, multicast does not work well over distances. Multicast can be enabled by navigating to **Distribution point** | **Multicast**.

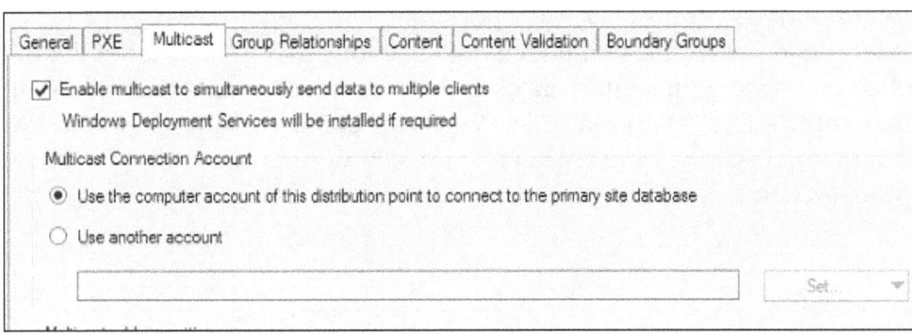

It is important to remember that Hyper-V 2012 has two types of network adapters, one legacy that supports PXE-boot and a synthetic adapter which does not support PXE-boot. With the release of Windows Server 2012 R2, Microsoft introduces a new generation virtual machine, called generation 2. This new virtual machine includes a totally new virtual hardware stack which includes UEFI boot and a synthetic network adapter that supports PXE boot and 10 GB networking.

Endpoint Protection

Endpoint Protection is an important feature, but if not properly configured will slow down much of your services. A common company might have different servers which host different services, such as e-mail servers, terminal servers, and file servers. These different services require different policies with regard to endpoint protection. With Configuration Manager, Microsoft has created a set of different standard policies, such as:

- IIS
- Exchange
- Terminal server (RDS)
- File servers
- SQL servers

These should be applied accordingly in order to make sure that endpoint protection does not slow down the performance of, for instance, SQL. You can import these templates by navigating to **Assets and Compliance** | **Endpoint protection** | **antimalware policies**. Right-click and choose import, then you will get a list of different template policies. If you have another application that you are unsure of what policy you need, you should check if the producer has an antivirus exclusion list for that application. As an example, Windows CRM, as shown in the following screenshot (`http://blogs.msdn.com/b/crminthefield/archive/2011/01/24/anti-virus-exclusions-for-microsoft-dynamics-crm.aspx`):

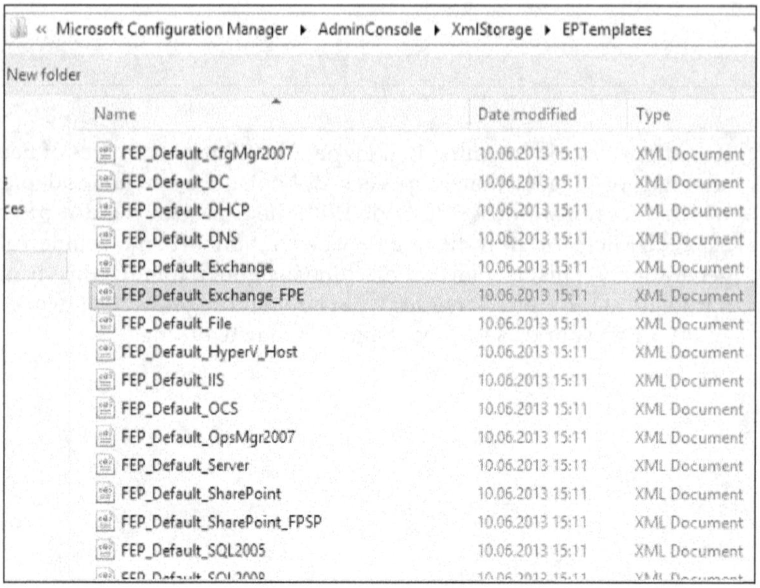

It is also important to note the endpoint policy precedence; if a computer is part of multiple collections that have endpoint policies set, the policy with the lowest priority wins. With Service Pack 1, there are some changes to this rule. When there are multiple antimalware policies that are deployed to the same client computer, they are merged on the client. When two settings are in conflict, the highest priority option is used. Some settings are also merged, such as exclusion lists from separate antimalware policies. Client-side merge also honors the priority that you configured for each antimalware policy.

> It is important to note that you should create your own collection if you have servers that host a particular service, since you need to deploy an antimalware policy to a collection. Also, you should always test the policies on a single server before deploying them to the rest of the servers, and be sure that real-time protection is turned off if you are unsure

The Configuration Manager site

Configuration Manager is highly dependent on its site's database, and therefore, it is important to keep the database clean and consistent and to speed up the performance of queries to the database. We can use maintenance tasks to remove stale and inactive entries. Most of these maintenance tasks are enabled by default and can be found by navigating to **Sites** | **Site Maintance**.

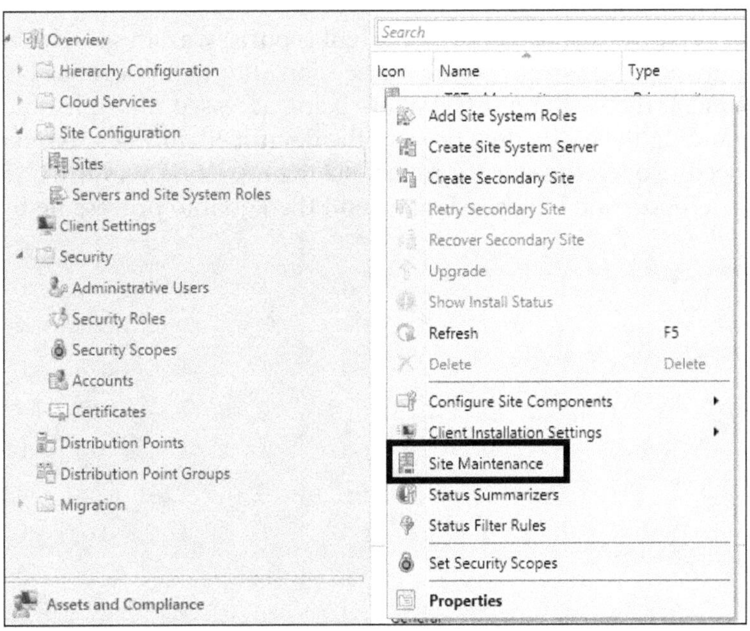

As we can see, there are multiple tasks that delete aged content from the database, and most of these "delete" tasks remove data that are marked as inactive. One of the tasks, called Rebuild indexes, is not enabled by default, and what it does is that it creates database indexes on the database columns that are at least 50 percent unique, and drops indexes on columns that are less than 50 percent unique and rebuilds all the existing indexes within the site's database. Important thing to note is that indexing a database table makes it much more efficient to run queries against it, which will increase performance on the site. Also, you have some of the other tasks that aren't enabled by default, which are **Delete Inactive Client Discovery Data** and **Delete Obsolete Client Discovery Data**. If we enable these two maintenance tasks, we need to configure them to run at a greater interval than the heartbeat discovery schedule. The reason for this is that then a client can send a heartbeat correctly; if not, the maintenance task will delete the record. Besides the maintenance tasks, it is important to remember that the lower the schedule we put on policy fetching and collection evaluations and such, the more load we will put on the SQL server. So, if we are having trouble with performance on the SQL server and we have 200 dynamic collections with a low collection evaluation, we should try to reevaluate our collections.

Reporting services

Reporting services should always run on a dedicated server since it consumes a lot of memory and CPU when generating reports. In most cases, the reporting service instance and the reporting server database should also be separated on different servers since this will give us a better performance.

In order to increase performance on individual reports, we can specify that it should be cached in memory. This allows faster execution after the report has been run for the first time. If there are reports that are being accessed multiple times a day, consider expanding the cache time beyond the default 30 minutes. To enable this feature, we need to open the specific report via the reporting server web service then right-click on a report and choose **Manage** and then go into processing options.

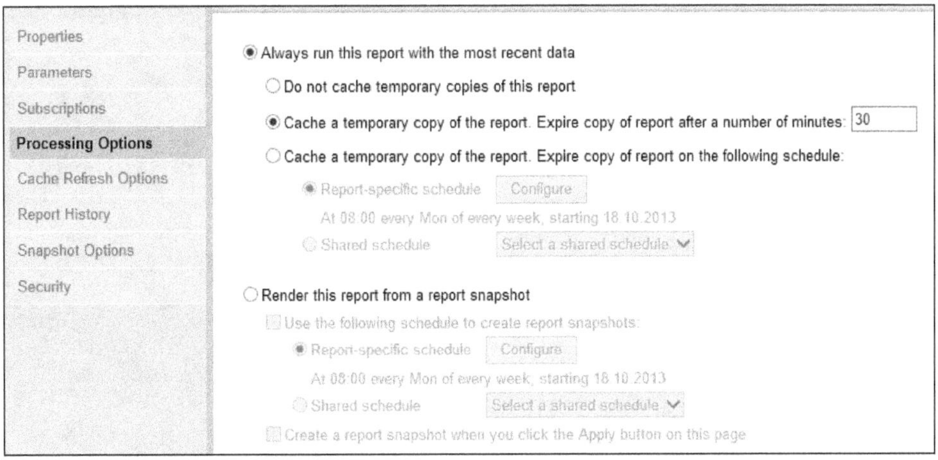

> There are some complaints that running the reports directly from the reporting server web service is a lot faster than running it directly from the Configuration Manager console.

Summary

We have now gone through the different components within Configuration Manager and what we can do to gain performance. We also had a look at how to identify bottlenecks and how to identify if our solution is set up according to Microsoft best practices. We also looked at how we could gain optimal performance by configuring other components, such as SQL.

Microsoft has done a good job as it has, out of the box, configured to deliver the best performance, and it makes it a lot easier with the latest release of Windows Server and System Center, but there is always room for improvement. Now this was the last chapter and hopefully, this has been a good learning experience for you as it has been for me.

Index

A

B

C

D

E

F

H

I

M

N

O

P

R

S

T

U

V

W

[PACKT] enterprise
professional expertise distilled
PUBLISHING

Thank you for buying
Microsoft System Center Configuration Manager
High availability and performance tuning

About Packt Publishing

Packt, pronounced 'packed', published its first book "Mastering phpMyAdmin for Effective MySQL Management" in April 2004 and subsequently continued to specialize in publishing highly focused books on specific technologies and solutions.

Our books and publications share the experiences of your fellow IT professionals in adapting and customizing today's systems, applications, and frameworks. Our solution based books give you the knowledge and power to customize the software and technologies you're using to get the job done. Packt books are more specific and less general than the IT books you have seen in the past. Our unique business model allows us to bring you more focused information, giving you more of what you need to know, and less of what you don't.

Packt is a modern, yet unique publishing company, which focuses on producing quality, cutting-edge books for communities of developers, administrators, and newbies alike. For more information, please visit our website: `www.packtpub.com`.

About Packt Enterprise

In 2010, Packt launched two new brands, Packt Enterprise and Packt Open Source, in order to continue its focus on specialization. This book is part of the Packt Enterprise brand, home to books published on enterprise software – software created by major vendors, including (but not limited to) IBM, Microsoft and Oracle, often for use in other corporations. Its titles will offer information relevant to a range of users of this software, including administrators, developers, architects, and end users.

Writing for Packt

We welcome all inquiries from people who are interested in authoring. Book proposals should be sent to author@packtpub.com. If your book idea is still at an early stage and you would like to discuss it first before writing a formal book proposal, contact us; one of our commissioning editors will get in touch with you.

We're not just looking for published authors; if you have strong technical skills but no writing experience, our experienced editors can help you develop a writing career, or simply get some additional reward for your expertise.

[PACKT] enterprise
professional expertise distilled
PUBLISHING

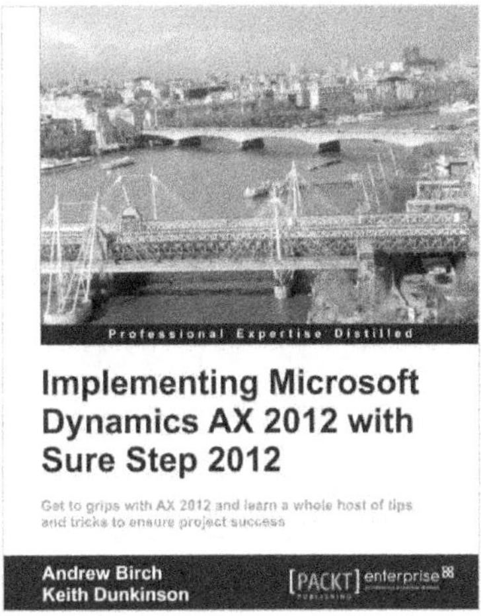

Implementing Microsoft Dynamics AX 2012 with Sure Step 2012

ISBN: 978-1-84968-704-1 Paperback: 234 pages

Get to grips with AX 2012 and learn a whole host of tips and tricks to ensure project success

1. Get the confidence to implement AX 2012 projects effectively using the Sure Step 2012 Methodology

2. Packed with practical real-world examples as well as helpful diagrams and images that make learning easier for you

3. Dive deep into AX 2012 to learn key technical 1. concepts to implement and manage a project

---

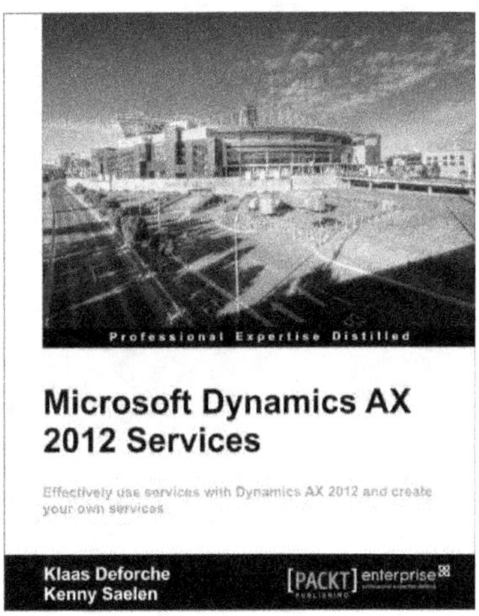

Microsoft Dynamics AX 2012 Services

ISBN: 978-1-84968-754-6 Paperback: 196 pages

Effectively use services with Dynamics AX 2012 and create your own services

1. Learn about the Dynamics AX 2012 service architecture.

2. Create your own services using wizards or X++ code

3. Consume existing web services and services you've created yourself

Please check **www.PacktPub.com** for information on our titles

www.ingramcontent.com/pod-product-compliance
Lightning Source LLC
LaVergne TN
LVHW082344200926
848481LV00012B/3451

* 9 7 8 1 7 8 2 1 7 6 7 6 3 *